Digital Souls

ALSO AVAILABLE FROM BLOOMSBURY

Being Posthuman: Ontologies of the Future, Zahi Zalloua
Haunted Data: Affect, Transmedia, Weird Science, Lisa Blackman
*The Meaning of Life and Death: Ten Classic Thinkers
on the Ultimate Question*, Michael Hauskeller

DIGITAL SOULS

A Philosophy of Online Death

Patrick Stokes

BLOOMSBURY ACADEMIC
LONDON • NEW YORK • OXFORD • NEW DELHI • SYDNEY

BLOOMSBURY ACADEMIC
Bloomsbury Publishing Plc
50 Bedford Square, London, WC1B 3DP, UK
1385 Broadway, New York, NY 10018, USA

BLOOMSBURY, BLOOMSBURY ACADEMIC and the Diana logo are trademarks of Bloomsbury Publishing Plc

First published in Great Britain 2021

Copyright © Patrick Stokes, 2021

Patrick Stokes has asserted his right under the Copyright, Designs and Patents Act, 1988, to be identified as Author of this work.

For legal purposes the Acknowledgements on p. vi constitute an extension of this copyright page.

Cover design by Charlotte Daniels
Cover image: © agsandrew / Getty Images

All rights reserved. No part of this publication may be reproduced or transmitted in any form or by any means, electronic or mechanical, including photocopying, recording, or any information storage or retrieval system, without prior permission in writing from the publishers.

Bloomsbury Publishing Plc does not have any control over, or responsibility for, any third-party websites referred to or in this book. All internet addresses given in this book were correct at the time of going to press. The author and publisher regret any inconvenience caused if addresses have changed or sites have ceased to exist, but can accept no responsibility for any such changes.

A catalogue record for this book is available from the British Library.

A catalog record for this book is available from the Library of Congress.

ISBN:	HB:	978-1-3501-3914-5
	PB:	978-1-3501-3915-2
	ePDF:	978-1-3501-3917-6
	eBook:	978-1-3501-3916-9

Typeset by Integra Software Private Limited

To find out more about our authors and books visit www.bloomsbury.com and sign up for our newsletters.

Contents

Acknowledgements vi

Introduction 1

1 Dying online 17

2 Online identity 31

3 Presence 53

4 Electric corpses 69

5 Second death 93

6 When the dead speak 123

7 Prey to the living 147

Coda: Mind uploads? 163

Notes 167
Index 191

Acknowledgements

This book is aimed at a general readership. For those seeking some more technical detail, I develop a number of the ideas discussed here in the following places:

- 'Ghosts in the Machine: Do the Dead Live on in Facebook?', *Philosophy and Technology* 25, no. 3 (2011): 363–79.
- 'Deletion as Second Death: The Moral Status of Digital Remains', *Ethics and Information Technology* 17, no. 4 (2015): 237–48.
- 'Death and Survival Online', in *Exploring the Philosophy of Death and Dying*, ed. Michael Cholbi and Travis Timmerman (London: Routledge, 2020).
- 'The Decay of Digital Personhood: Towards New Norms of Disposal and Preservation', in *Residues of Death: Disposal Refigured*, ed. Tamara Kohn, Martin Gibbs, Bjorn Nansen and Luke van Ryn (London: Routledge, 2019): 80–90.

My interest in this topic started while I was a Marie Curie Intra-European Fellow at the University of Hertfordshire, 2010–12, funded by the European Commission. I'm grateful to John Lippitt for his encouragement and help over many years, and to my colleagues at UH at the time, especially Brendan Larvor, Luciano Floridi and Dan Hutto.

My colleagues at Deakin, both past and present, have likewise been enormously supportive. My thanks to Sean Bowden, Petra Brown, Leesa Davis, George Duke, Russell Grigg, Stan van Hooft, Douglas Kirsner, Helen Ngo, Jack Reynolds, Jon Roffe, Matthew Sharpe and Marilyn Stendera, and to Matthew Clarke, Fethi Mansouri and Brenda Cherednichenko for their support.

Students past and present have helped shape and challenge my thinking on these topics. Thanks in particular to Brodie Kennelly, Tim Neal, Trisha Villagonzalo and Amra Copcic for our discussions of technology and the dead, and to Neil Henderson for his valuable research assistance.

In grappling with the philosophy of death, Adam Buben has been a constant companion and collaborator for well over a decade now. Our many discussions, as well as his feedback and advice, have been indispensable. His karaoke remains appalling.

I'm grateful to audiences at the University of Hertfordshire, California State Polytechnic University Pomona, Deakin University, University College Dublin and Monash University, as well as the Victorian Humanists Society, the Existentialist Society and the University of the Third Age; to members of the Death Online Research Network who have shared many useful pieces of information among the group; and to all those who have, whether they remember it or not, helped or influenced this project: Megan Altman, Roman Altshuler, Michael Arnold, Don Arthur, Emily Baxter, Jason Brown, Michael Cholbi, Martin Gibbs, Margaret Gibson, Elaine Kasket, Tamara Kohn, Bjorn Nansen, Marya Schechtman, Travis Timmerman, John Troyer, Luke van Ryn and to all those people who, when they heard what I was working on, have generously shared their own digital bereavement stories with me over the years.

Finally, thanks to my friends and family for their support and encouragement, and to Jess, in every way, always.

Introduction

An email from Jack

Tim Hart was sitting on his couch one evening in November 2011 when he got an email with the subject line 'I'm watching'. The message was short and to the point:

> Did you hear me? I'm at your house. Clean your fucking attic!!!
>
> –
>
> Jack Fröse

Jack Froese had been a close friend of Hart's since their teens. They'd been inseparable for seventeen years. A few months earlier Froese and Hart had been up in Hart's attic at his home in Dunmore, Pennsylvania. Jack had teased him then about how messy it was; now, it seemed, he was doing it again.

Except Jack was dead.

That June, Froese had died suddenly of a heart arrhythmia, at the obscenely young age of thirty-two. Months later, he started emailing people. Those who replied to these emails never got a response, and the messages stopped as abruptly as they began.

Not long after Froese's death, a group of philosophers gathered in a seminar room on the other side of the Atlantic to hear David

Oderberg offer a curious thought experiment: what if you received an anonymous email, containing information that you *and you alone* were privy to? In Oderberg's example, imagine getting an email stating that 'I know you felt like killing Mr Watson for failing you on your A-level English exam' – something you'd never told anyone at all – 'but you deserved to fail'.[1] Who has this message come from: God? Your future self, somehow? A spambot whose random message just happened, by mind-boggling coincidence, to describe your early life? The late Mr Watson, now posthumously aware of how you felt that day and eager to set the record straight?

For the specific purpose of the interaction, says Oderberg, it doesn't really matter, just as when a solider receives an order on the battlefield it doesn't matter whether the order comes from the colonel or the general. Both options have what Oderberg dubs 'telic possibility'. Something is telically possible if it *might as well have been true*.[2] The order, insofar as its function is to command an action, might as well have come from the colonel as from the general: an order is an order. We might care about who the sender was for other reasons, of course. Maybe the soldier is worried about how wise the order is, in which case the fact that the colonel is a tactical genius while the general is an incompetent buffoon is surely relevant. But as it's an order, and so must be followed regardless, this makes no practical difference.

Not infrequently, according to Oderberg, electronic communication is just like this. If all you want is to know how to drive to the nearest supermarket, GPS navigation with synthesized speech is just as effective as a human sitting next to you with a roadmap. Someone who was under the misapprehension there was a flesh-and-blood person on the other end of the SatNav reading out driving instructions to them in real time would get to their destination just as quickly as someone who understands they're listening to a computer. The voice might as well be a person as a piece of software.

I don't, in fact, think the emails from Jack Froese's account rise to the level of the Mr Watson example that Oderberg gives – an example which itself is not, as Oderberg notes, watertight, though it can easily be made so with a few modifications. There are other plausible, earthly explanations for Jack's emails, though not all of them ultimately check out. For instance, you *can* send an email after you die, if you've done a bit of planning. There are online services specifically designed to send pre-prepared messages on your behalf after your death. Some rely on a next of kin contacting the service to let them know the user has died. Others require the user to log in at set intervals or reply to periodic emails, and will assume the user has died if they don't respond. (So if you're keen to use such a service to tell people how much you secretly hated, cheated on or lusted after them, just make sure you don't fall into a long coma and then wake up. Things could get awkward.) That would be a very neat explanation for Froese's emails – except that the email his cousin Jimmy McGraw received mentions an injury that happened long *after* Froese had died:

> Hey Jim, How ya doing? I knew you were gonna break your ankle, tried to warn you. Gotta be careful.
> Tell Rock for me, Great song, huh? Your [*sic*] welcome.
> Couldn't get through to him. His [email address] email didn't work
>   – Jack Fröse

So much for the idea of pre-prepared emails, at least in this case. (It's also good to know even the dead get email bouncebacks sometimes.) What seems more likely is that someone with access to Froese's account sent the emails, perhaps as part of their grieving process. But what's really interesting here is not how the emails came about, but the responses of the people who got them. Hart's attitude was that, even if someone other than Jack wrote the emails, it ultimately doesn't matter:

> We looked into it a little bit [...] we spoke to his mother, and she told us, you know, 'Think what you want about it, or just accept it as a gift,' which I did. And if somebody's messing around, I don't care because I take it whatever way I want.

Likewise, Froese's mother Patty focused on the consequences of the emails rather than their origin:

> The emails that people had received, I thought they were fantastic, they were great. I saw, you know, they made people happy, upset some people, but to me that's keeping people talking about him.[3]

In other words, to use Oderberg's language, Froese's friends and family treated it as telically possible that the emails were from Jack. For the purpose of the communication, it didn't really matter. They had the emails, and felt comforted by a sense of Jack's persistence, whatever their origin.

Beyond the supernatural

That may seem more than passing strange. If you got an email from a dead person, surely the most pressing question is whether it's really from them or not? Such an email, if genuine, would be proof of life after death. The implications are barely even thinkable. Every aspect of our lives, from physics to religion to the very structure of society, would be transformed.

Yet when it comes to things supernatural, once you stop asking 'is it real?', a number of other questions, perhaps more interesting and certainly more productive, come into view. For instance, people have been reporting seeing UFOs for over seventy years – a fact that becomes far richer and more illuminating when you stop wondering about flesh-and-blood extraterrestrials and start looking at the feedback loops between Cold War anxieties, pop culture and folklore. As Susan Lepselter puts it in her haunting ethnography of life among UFO 'experiencers', *The Resonance of Unseen Things*, these experiences can 'reveal both biological and phenomenological experience, and social as well as individual meaning' regardless of whether they 'really happened' or not.[4] Likewise, 'Do ghosts exist?' is ultimately a less rewarding question than 'What does ghost belief and experience tell us about ourselves?' The historian Owen Davies notes that English ghosts originally tended to be the spirits of the recently dead, but started to appear from the deeper past as the public's knowledge of history increased. (Ghostly Roman legionaries, for example, didn't start showing up until the twentieth century.)[5] Either that's an inexplicable fact about the supernatural, or it's a fascinating indication of how folklore is tied to and conditioned by the current knowledge of the folk. The same goes for all those Venusians and Martians reported by 'contactees' in the 1950s, before space probes showed the public how lifeless those planets are – whereupon aliens from further afield suddenly started to arrive.

So for our purposes at least, whether or not Jack Froese really is sending emails from beyond the grave is beside the point. The truly compelling aspect of this story is what it tells us about our relationship with the dead, and with technology. Jack Froese left his friends in Dunmore, and yet never did. He was both painfully absent and yet inescapably present. Our world is haunted, not by actual ghosts – whose traditional transparency is symbolic of their ambiguity, of both being and not-being, alive and dead, visible and immaterial all at once – but by those we loved and love.

This has always been how we have lived with the dead. They persist everywhere and nowhere, from the solidity of corpses to wispy traces in dreams, writing, buildings and even in the faces of their descendants. From the ancestor mask processions of the Romans through to the death masks of the royal and famous that began to be produced during the late Middle Ages, from the earliest portraiture to photography and video, humans have found ways to preserve the *phenomenality* of the dead, the distinctive way they appear and sound. Jack Froese's emails are perhaps best seen as part of that tradition, whoever sent them. Yet they are also an example of the more striking, more invasive ways in which technology allows the face, the voice, the very presence of the dead to persist like never before.

There is something troubling here, too. In treating the possibility that they were communicating with Froese as a telic one – the emails *might as well* have come from Froese as from someone else – the recipients of these emails risk doing him a kind of unintentional disrespect. (Imagine someone receiving a love letter and declaring 'A letter from my beloved! Or possibly someone pretending to be them. Doesn't matter either way, really, so long as it's a good letter!'.) The emails that reveal both Jack's ongoing presence in the life of those who loved him and his irreparable absence from that world, also serve to preserve Jack even as they threaten to overwrite or replace him at the same time.

So the curious story of Jack Froese captures two key themes we'll return to again and again throughout our journey into the electric afterlife: the way in which new technologies allow the dead to persist among us in enhanced ways, and the way in which they risk turning the dead into mere fodder for the living. Danger lies in the very thing that makes electronic communication so powerful: the transparency of the medium, the frictionless ease with which others appear to us, unburdened by distance and delay. As the internet folds itself into the sinews of our everyday existence, as our flesh becomes increasingly digitized, the gap between electronic and face-to-face communication is closing. As we'll see, that makes it far easier for the dead to remain among the living. But it can also change our relationship to the dead in ethically troubling ways. With every day that passes the internet fills up more and more with dead people, while our ability to reanimate them becomes ever more powerful. The dead are both more robust and more vulnerable – and we're not ready for any of this. We need, urgently, to understand what the internet era means for our relationship to the dead, and what new demands this makes of us. To do this, we first need to confront a startling question, at once frightening, exhilarating and absurd: *does the internet let us survive death?*

Electric are the dead

New forms of communication technology are always sold to us with a certain breathless enthusiasm: *the future is here!* So it's easy to lose sight of the fact that electric communication is now in its third century, reckoning from Francis Roland's first working telegraph of 1816, two decades before Samuel Morse. What's perhaps even more remarkable is that, as the cultural historian Jeffrey Sconce demonstrates in his book *Haunted Media*, the idea of communicating with the dead became conceptually entangled with electric communication right from the start.[6] Commercial telegraph services began to appear at roughly the same moment as the table-turning craze, which began with the rapping 'spirits' that plagued the Fox Sisters in Hydesville, New York, in 1848. The uncanny new technology of communication-at-a-distance provided a helpful structuring metaphor: the electric telegraph allowed the living to speak to each other across vast distances, while the 'spiritual telegraph' of the séance room bridged the gulf between the living and the dead.

This 'spiritual telegraph' metaphor was not simply about the instantaneous crossing of vast distance either, but also about the force that made this possible. By the late 1860s the events at Hydesville were already being interpreted in explicitly electrical language.[7] Nor was this a wholly American phenomenon. A few years ago I found myself working on some strange old pamphlets held in the Royal Library in Copenhagen.[8] The pamphlets, written under pen names such as 'Mensa mobilis' and 'Dr Practicus', dated to the arrival of table-turning (*borddansen*, 'the table dance') in Denmark, which seems to have hit in earnest around April 1853.[9] 'Copenhagen has become as if *electrified*', according to one such pamphlet; 'wherever one goes, people speak only of *borddandsen*'.[10] The unknown authors of these pamphlets offer practical advice on table-turning and speculate about the mysterious 'heretofore hidden power'[11] behind it. To describe this power, the authors draw upon the earlier language of mesmerism, a pseudoscientific belief system that riffed on the emerging science of electricity. The mesmerists believed in a vitalist 'animal magnetism' or 'magnetic fluid' which, when skilfully manipulated, could produce exotic hypnosis-like effects as well as curing various ailments. 'Mensa mobilis' draws on this mesmerist vocabulary in suggesting that 'Animal Thermo-Electricity' moves the *borddansen* table, and that this 'current' can be insulated with glass,[12] while Dr Practicus recommends that female sitters 'hold the current in' by wearing silk.[13]

This suspicion that communicating with the dead was somehow electrical in character flowed, so to speak, both ways. When Congress debated whether to fund Morse's experiments in telegraphy, Congressman Cave Johnson demanded, perhaps mockingly, that some of the funding be instead used for experiments in mesmerism; the committee chair said it was, indeed, important to determine scientifically if telegraphy and mesmerism were related.[14] When Walt Whitman declared 'I sing the body electric' in 1867 he was simultaneously saying something shockingly new and drawing on established associations between electricity, corporeality and spirituality.[15]

In fact, the telegraph as we know it may itself be a work of mourning. In 1825 Samuel Morse had been painting a commissioned portrait of the Marquis de Lafayette in Washington, DC, when a horse messenger brought word from New York that Morse's wife Lucretia was ill. The next day another message arrived to say Lucretia had died. Morse left immediately, but by the time he got home Lucretia had already been buried.[16] We cannot say – though this has never stopped people from speculating – to what extent this tragedy inspired Morse to overcome the problem of communication over distance. What we can say is that the problems of delayed communication and death were lived, painful parts of Morse's experience, and that his invention became, due to surprising historical contingencies, bound up in the cultural imaginary with the idea of an invisible world beyond.

That association of the dead with electric communication, as Sconce notes, lingered right throughout the twentieth century. Near the end of his life, Thomas Edison was speculating to reporters about the possibility of building a machine so sensitive it could communicate with the dead.[17] Both Edison and Alexander Graham Bell, inventor of the telephone, experimented with telepathy by winding wires around people's heads.[18] (It didn't work.) Many people found the telephone unsettling and even creepy the first time they heard it, reminiscent of the mysterious disembodied voices of the séance room. In particular, the entirely new phenomenon of white noise unnerved early telephone users; some came to interpret these sounds as somehow connected to or even communications from the afterlife.[19]

While 'spirit photography' had been a widespread practice since William Mumler began imposing the ghostly faces of Civil War soldiers onto portraits of their grieving families in New York, attempts to record the dead using electronic audio techniques had to wait for the reel-to-reel tape recorder to make its way into homes and businesses. (Though as Tony Walter points out, Nipper, the dog on the 'His Master's Voice' phonograph label, was sometimes taken to be listening to his *dead* master's voice.)[20] When Swedish painter and film director Friedrich Jürgenson listened back to his birdsong recordings in 1959 and heard what he came to interpret as the voices of the dead, he inaugurated the 'Electronic Voice Phenomena' (EVP) that continue to this day.[21] According to one, possibly apocryphal account, on the day of Jürgenson's funeral a colleague deliberately turned a TV onto a vacant channel – and sure enough, Jürgenson's face appeared in the static.[22]

Disembodied voices on tape, haunted televisions and tropes about electric communication with the hereafter all exist in the rich folkloric background of Jack Froese's emails. Electronic media collapses time and space, removes the tyranny of distance and absence; understandable, then, that overcoming the *ultimate* distance and the *final* absence, the chasm that separates us from the dead, would come to figure in the cultural imagination of the first generations of humans to live with this new technology. But this book is not about the supernatural. It's about the everyday and mundane. The dead do not just appear to us in terrifying visions or mysterious cyphers, but in the very real material and mental traces they leave behind. Haunting is an everyday event, not an anomalous one. And with the digital age, the dead have found new ways to haunt us more comprehensively than ever before.

Stay on the line

On a hill just outside of the town of Otsuchi, in Japan's northern Iwate Prefecture, stands an old phone booth, painted white. Inside is a disconnected rotary dial phone. Local artist Itaru Sasaki installed the

'Wind Phone' in 2010 as a way of grieving for his cousin. No longer able to talk on a real telephone line, he wanted his thoughts to be carried instead on the wind. The following March, much of Otsuchi was wiped out by the tsunami that followed the magnitude 9.0 Tōhoku earthquake, an event that killed over sixteen thousand people nationally. One in every ten people living in Otsuchi died; nearly half of these victims were never found. The Wind Phone, high on its hill, was spared.

Today, visitors from Otsuchi and far beyond walk up the hill to speak to their dead loved ones on the Wind Phone. Sachiko Okawa, whose husband died in the disaster, regularly comes to the Wind Phone with her grandsons to talk to him: 'Hi Grandpa. How are you? I'll be in fourth grade next semester. Wasn't that fast?' Kikue Hirano dials the number of the last house she and her husband shared in Otsuchi; both he and the house were carried off by the tsunami. She dials, but says nothing. Other callers are far more plaintive. 'I'm so sorry I couldn't save you.' 'Without all of you, it's meaningless.' 'Why did you die? Why did it have to be you, dad?'[23]

Talking to the dead this way is, no doubt, as old as grief itself. The form may be new (even if a bit self-consciously retro), but the activity is a familiar one. The Wind Phone provides what philosophers of mind, psychologists and theorists of technology call an *affordance*, a possibility for an engagement between the self and its environment. The handle of a coffee mug, for instance, presents the affordance of holding the mug comfortably while drinking it. A landline telephone presents the affordance of talking to those not present. The affordance of the Wind Phone is to speak, safely and freely, to the dead, to unburden yourself of some of what you carry. Alone in a booth, with a familiar piece of comfortingly old technology begging in its very form to be spoken into, people are afforded the chance to speak, often in ways they could never speak to the living.

As we'll see, untold numbers of social media users perform precisely this same act of one-way communication with the dead every day. They do not need to make the pilgrimage to the Wind Phone, or even to the cemetery, however. Aware that others are watching, they may not always speak with the frankness of those wrestling with their loss in the confessional privacy of the Wind Phone. Yet they speak. They speak to the dead. And in so doing, as we'll see, they both preserve the dead among the living, and yet also risk effacing them.

The Wind Phone only 'works' one-way. It's a 'prop' in the sense in which the philosopher Kendall Walton uses the term: a real-world object that makes certain propositions true in a make-believe world.[24] In the hands of a child, a real-world broom can make it true-in-a-make-believe-world that the child is riding a horse. In the Wind Phone, you enter a make-believe world in which the dead are on the line, taking in your words. The phone – disconnected, inert, literally powerless – makes it true-in-the-make-believe world that you're talking to the dead and not merely talking to yourself in a wood and glass box. There are, however, other ways of using a phone to engage the dead in which phones function not as props but as prostheses.

Aaron Purmont lives in his widow's phone. His son Ralph only knows Aaron through the videos and photos he sees there:

> My phone is my time machine, and the cool blue light that is undoubtedly destroying my circadian rhythms helps me slip easily into another life, the one where I'm 28 and recklessly, heedlessly in love with a man who makes me Robyn mix CDs and leaves them in my car. The one where I'm 29 again and pregnant with the baby the doctors told me not to have but who I knew would keep my husband alive a little bit longer. Or the one where I'm 31 again, carrying the man I love down the hallway to the bathroom, staying up at night to hear his breath, knowing someday I would miss that gentle sound.[25]

Nora McInerney Purmont's words are hard to read. They are suffused with the ambiguous temporality of grief, of a loved one that is both present and absent, a past both inescapable and irrecoverable. She writes with unbearable concreteness, in flashes of memory that are both 'in-the-moment' and set within a larger narrative that colours every detail with poignancy. Anyone who has lost anyone knows the way memories come at you in this rich, fragmented, saturated way. Nora's phone, in that sense, is an extension of her 'organic' memory of Aaron, a way of calling up these past moments and producing rushes of recollection and recognition. It's also what Alison Landsberg has dubbed a 'prosthetic memory', a media device that brings other people (in this case, Ralph, who was less than two years old when his father died) into memories of events they did not experience themselves.[26] In that, the phone is just the latest in the long line of aides humans have always used to keep the phenomenality of the dead present with us. We have always drawn portraits, carved statues, kept handwriting and locks of hair, all tools for buttressing the memories of those who knew the dead and presenting them anew to those who did not. The technology may be recent, but the task itself is a recognizably ancient one.

But there's something new here too. The internet – arguably the largest human-made artefact ever[27] – changes our experience of time.[28] In particular, it collapses all moments into a sort of eternal present. When all moments of history are accessible via online search, all moments of time are equidistant, with any moment the same number of clicks away from us as any other. Thanks to Google, anyone can call up an image of Aaron as fast as they can any other person. In Nora's engagement with Aaron's online traces, it's all there all at once: the mix tapes and the pregnancy and the travel photos and the chemotherapy. In 1998, the Spanish government ran newspaper ads for the forced sale of two properties due to social security debts, one of which was owned by Mario Costeja González. A decade later, Costeja González complained to the newspaper and then to Google that the first result when someone searched on his name was that old forced sale announcement. The search engine, he argued, was keeping this past financial embarrassment alive unfairly and damaging his reputation unjustly. The case led all the way to a landmark Court of Justice of the European Union ruling that established a new legal right, phrased resonantly if paradoxically as the 'right to be forgotten'. (Paradoxical, if we assume that rights create duties, and that duties can be carried out: how do we *deliberately* forget? How can we be blamed for *failing* to forget something?) But it was the temporality of the internet that was part of the problem here; not just its refusal to forget, but its structural inability to let events retreat into the past, to give the present its privileged place.

These two phone examples – one 'old' disconnected technology used as a prop, one 'new' technology used to access a network – point to an interplay of old and new that we'll be seeing throughout this book. Our online engagement with death and the dead ranges from novelties like apps that helpfully remind you you're going to die one day to new forms of global grief and the prospect of new uses and abuses of the dead. How much of this is genuinely new, and how much simply extends our existing relationship with the dead? And what does new technology show us about death *itself* that was perhaps not obvious before?

The task for philosophy

Sociologists, psychologists and internet studies theorists have been quick to notice the ways in which the internet is changing our relationship to death. Online mourning practices, from taking selfies at funerals to holding in-game memorials and building in-game mausoleums, have caught the eye of researchers from a range of academic disciplines. Anyone wanting to explore the landscape of digital death now has extensive research to draw upon.

Philosophers, however, have been much slower to turn their attention to this topic. There are probably several reasons for this. One may be residual snobbishness about doing 'applied' philosophy, though this seems to be far less prevalent in the profession now. Another is that philosophy is, by its nature, a slow-moving beast. Academic philosophers write books and papers that take years to appear, which makes it hard to say anything too specific about social phenomena that change rapidly. (I wrote my first paper on the topic of digital death in 2011; half the websites I mentioned by name in that paper are now moribund or defunct.) When Hubert Dreyfus wrote his book *On the Internet* in 2001 he argued that the internet simply contained too much data for meaningful information search to be possible. In 2008 he published a second edition in which he had to admit he'd gotten that wrong. Google happened.[29] No doubt a similar fate awaits this book.

Yet this is a topic ripe for philosophical exploration. Ancient questions about the metaphysical and ethical status of the dead collide with new ones about our relationship to our information and our ownership of digital property. Anxieties about whether public grief is 'real' and who has the right to grieve are amplified when mourning is instantaneous and global. And, as I'll try to show, emerging distinctions in the literature between *persons* as social objects and *selves* as first-personal subjects, as well as related questions of otherness and consciousness, come into sharper focus as we consider looming new forms of posthumous survival. Crucially, this is not just an academic concern, but an urgent practical one. How are we to meet the ontological and ethical challenges of the world that is coming into view? Can people *really* survive death online? Should we let them?

I should be clear here about what this book is, and what it isn't. I am not a psychologist, nor a media studies researcher, nor a philosopher of media. My interest is instead as a philosopher of death and of personal identity. That focus pushes the discussion in a particular direction, but the topic unavoidably calls for a wider intellectual net than academics, being specialists, are typically comfortable with. In this book we will draw upon a range of philosophical traditions and literatures without being beholden to any one of them. We will draw on empirical and theoretical findings from a range of disciplines. We will hear voices from all three centuries of the electric era to help us make sense of how we live with the dead now.

We can expect a few run-ins with the uncanny along the way. When I was in the early stages of writing this, the Australian journalist Mark Colvin died, aged sixty-five. A universally admired broadcaster and author, Colvin was also an avid and highly responsive Twitter user. The news broke around 11:40 am, and Twitter was immediately flooded with tributes. Then, at 1:18 pm, Colvin's account posted a single tweet:

It's all been bloody marvellous.

Was that sent by a family member on his behalf? Had he, knowing the end was near, scheduled the tweet? Was the ghost of Mark Colvin somehow using his iPhone?

Nobody, it seemed, felt like asking.[30] They all just wanted to say goodbye and explain what Colvin meant to them. It was what it was. 'Think what you want about it, or just accept it as a gift.'

1

Dying online

On the morning of 15 July 1974, Florida TV anchor Christine Chubbuck pulled out a handgun and shot herself live on air. She died in hospital several hours later. Footage of this tragedy reportedly still exists, but remains locked away in a law firm's safe. By contrast, footage of Pennsylvania Treasurer R. Budd Dwyer fatally shooting himself in front of a horrified press pack in January 1987 is never more than a couple of clicks away.

It's commonly said that dying, at least in the 'Global North', has become an increasingly private and hidden affair. Where once we died at home, and our bodies often stayed there until burial, from the early decades of the twentieth century onwards we increasingly died in hospitals.[1] Yet the internet has drastically changed the visibility of death, or at least of certain deaths. On Friday 15 March 2019, a white supremacist armed with assault weapons livestreamed himself entering two mosques in Christchurch and murdering fifty people. The New Zealand police asked media outlets not to show the livestream footage; many nonetheless did. Two days later, the website Reddit took down a subreddit (discussion page) called r/watchpeopledie for violating Reddit's 'policy against glorifying or encouraging violence', after it posted the gunman's footage.[2] This subreddit was known for displaying videos of gruesome deaths. In that, it was not unusual: websites such as the notorious Rotten.com had been displaying horrific footage of violent death and its aftermath since the mid-1990s. Access to such 'forbidden' imagery was one (thankfully small) part of the early internet's allure.

The deaths of Chubbuck and Dwyer were sufficiently shocking in their time and context that they are still discussed today. Broadcast deaths on the internet, tragically, are common enough that they are hardly reported. On the various livestreaming platforms now available, people broadcast their own self-inflicted deaths as well as their killing of other people. Even producing internet content can be deadly, as in 2017 when Pedro Ruiz was accidentally shot dead by his girlfriend on camera during a YouTube stunt gone wrong.[3]

At the same time as some deaths have become more visible, there has been increasing concern about the internet profaning or intruding upon grief and death. Barak Obama was criticized in some quarters for taking a selfie at Nelson Mandela's memorial service with the prime ministers of Denmark and the UK. You could put that down to the relentlessly partisan tribalism of our age, but the criticism also reflected anxieties over how we handle death in the social media era. Every so often an op-ed writer somewhere will decry the rise of selfies at funerals as tasteless or vapid; yet a study done on the use of '#funeral' on Instagram found most photos recorded the events of dressing formally or extended families being together, not the actual funeral service.[4] The photos 'appeared to be efforts to communicate and share feelings of intimacy, togetherness, family, friendship, and attachment' and 'celebrated the deceased's intimate and social connections and the community drawn together by the event of their passing'.[5] Relatively few selfies featured a coffin, let alone a corpse.

But complaints that selfies are inappropriate in the context of death rituals point to something else: the sense that the internet lacks the moral seriousness needed for moments of such gravity. Selfies are seen as frivolous, flippant, self-absorbed; everything death and grieving are not. Even in societies where the bodies of the dead are not typically hidden away, sharing images of bodies online strikes some people as wrong in something like the way that sharing videos of deaths is. In Samoa, where open-casket funerals are a cultural norm, photographs and videos of dead people's bodies are increasingly being shared on platforms like TikTok and Facebook – but some are starting to resist the trend. Samoans are used to visible corpses, yet using social media to extend that visibility feels to some Samoans at least like a violation of dignity.[6]

We can understand this concern about the dignity of the newly dead as akin to worries about nudity. J. David Velleman has argued that the reason we find the exposure of breasts and genitals (and male genitals in particular) shameful is that these parts, not being entirely within our control, remind us of our animal nature.[7] Few things speak to our animality more than a corpse: an organism shorn of mind, reduced to pure biological form and shape. Perhaps that's also one reason why footage of deaths upsets us so much: a feeling that the moment at which someone is reclaimed by their organic nature, reduced to matter, to mere object, is something outsiders should not be looking at.

Yet there's also the sense that by mediating and sharing these images, we somehow dilute their reality. We reduce the end of a life and the body that remains afterwards to just one more item in an economy of 'content' competing for our attention. Death becomes detached from the embodied reality we live in. As Nikolaus Lehner has recently put it, 'The reality of death and foremost, the reality of our own personal death and the death of our loved ones, strangely loses some of its significance because of this media environment. The images of death overwrite the imagination of death.'[8] It overwrites the one who has died, too. Just as Christine Chubbock and Budd Dwyer are forever defined by their last moments, dying online can, as it were, crowd out everything that came before.

In this 'attention economy', to share images or footage a particular death, far from driving home its dreadful reality, can just as easily level real and fictional deaths. Most of us have at some point been emotionally moved by the death of a fictional character, but the sort of levelling I'm talking about here makes it easy to treat *real* deaths as if they too are fictional. When Virginia journalist Alison Parker and her cameraman Adam Ward were shot dead on live TV in August 2015, a small but vocal subset of internet users insisted the deaths were staged. It's become surprisingly commonplace in the face of mass-casualty events, such as the Boston Marathon bombing and the Sandy Hook shooting, for conspiracy theorists to insist that the people on screen crying for their children or being rushed to hospital are just 'crisis actors' taking part in fake tragedies. One reason many of us find this so repugnant is precisely that real deaths – and accordingly real pain – are being handled as if they are just another image for consumption and critique.[9] Real-life tragedy and grisly fantasy are treated as being on the same level. Electronic media can bring death home to us, but it can also detach those deaths from reality altogether.

This points to one of the major hurdles to the idea of surviving death online: the sense that the online world is unreal, or at least less real. When it comes to death, that sense pervades not just the mediated deaths we see on our screens, but also the ways we mourn people online, and how we deal with cases of actual fakery that sometimes cross our path.

Online mourning and trolling

On 24 February 2012, just a week after the online public mourning of Whitney Houston, British comedian Michael Legge announced the death of 'Gregg Jevin, a man I just made up' – sparking an outbreak of mock grief. Twitter users lamented how impossible it was to imagine a world without Gregg Jevin in it, or wondered how they'd break the news to their also-imaginary children. Businesses and brands got into the action; even the BBC tweeted news of the death.[10] A few users even threw in the sort of predictable contrarian tweets that always follow celebrity deaths: for instance, 'Tory sell-out. Good riddance' by @mrmarksteel, or 'Oh please, spare me the orgy of false grief. Thousands of made-up people die every day and no-one tweets about them at all' by, uh, @patstokes.

The Gregg Jevin affair exposed something very interesting that perhaps wasn't obvious to Twitter users before: Twitter mourning as a practice was less than six years old, but people already knew its conventions well enough to parody them. We could only make these jokes because we knew what sincere Twitter grief looked like. But the existence of these jokes, and the way in which fairly mainstream, image-conscious organizations got involved, also suggests that online mourning was seen as fair game for satire, in a way that would likely be pointless or crass if directed at more familiar forms of public grief. What is it about *online* mourning that might make it seem a more deserving target for this sort of humour?

Researchers across a range of fields including sociology, psychology and anthropology have studied the nature of online mourning quite extensively. We'll touch on social media mourning practices a little later in this book, but online mourning is a much wider category than just social media. Mourning practices exist on platforms ranging from early web-based condolence books and online obituaries to elaborate Minecraft mausoleums and commemorative non-playable characters in massively multiplayer online roleplaying games (MMORPGs).[11] All of these throw up philosophically intriguing questions about identity, action and ethics; for instance, World of Warcraft players have found themselves caught up in fierce debates over the ethics of staging ambush attacks on in-game funerals, held for players who have died 'in real life'.[12]

While some forms of online mourning are extensions of pre-internet mourning practices, others are new. That in turn has allowed for some positive developments. Supportive communities of mourning can spring up in unexpected places, bringing together bereaved people who would never have met otherwise.[13] Even the video-sharing behemoth YouTube, a site not exactly known for its polite and supportive comment culture, has helped people dealing with loss to connect and draw strength from each other.[14] One thing the internet has been particularly helpful at is proving spaces for 'disenfranchised grief': grieving by people who are not entitled to mourn according to prevailing social standards or assumptions.[15] Grief might be viewed as illegitimate because of who is being mourned (a pet, for instance), or the mourner may not have the 'right' sort of relationship to the deceased (such as an extramarital partner). The online world creates new places for these excluded mourners to congregate and to express what they're feeling. The flipside of this, though, is that online mourning spaces can be also accessed by mourners who the bereaved may reasonably want to keep excluded, such as people involved in the death itself.[16]

When Gregg Jevin 'died', those of us who got into the game were play-acting what psychologists call 'parasocial grief'. A parasocial relationship is one-sided: you may consider yourself Adam Driver's biggest fan or a fervently devoted subject of the Queen, but neither, mostly likely, has ever heard of you.[17] Not all parasocial grief is directed towards celebrities, however. Non-famous people who die in high-profile accidents or murders can become the focus of online grieving even where none of the mourners had even heard of the deceased before they died.[18] Memorial Facebook pages, for instance, pop up and grow rapidly following a heavily publicized death, despite the page creators having no direct connection to the person they're mourning.

Parasocial grief can look bewildering, even absurd, to outsiders.[19] That in turn makes the mourner appear somehow suspect to onlookers: suspect rationally if they're grieving for an improper object of mourning, and morally if someone is seen as grandstanding or insinuating themselves into someone else's tragedy. On social media, that can lead to a degree of 'grief policing'. Some users will take it upon themselves to try to pull anyone into line who they see as mourning inappropriately – for instance by displaying 'excessive' sadness for someone they never knew personally, or getting upset about someone who is 'just' an actor or musician.[20] People who did in fact know the deceased personally can also become distressed by strangers assuming a too-easy intimacy.[21]

A more extreme and altogether more distressing response to parasocial grief is the practice of 'RIP trolling'. The term 'trolling' has mutated over the years, but in something close to its original sense it refers to an irony-soaked, self-consciously provocative (and often racist, misogynistic and homophobic) practice of online harassment. In RIP trolling, the troll(s) deliberately disrupts an online memorial space by posting offensive comments about the dead person, obscene imagery and so on. When twenty-year-old Oliva Burt died in an accident outside a Durham nightclub in February 2018, her family's pain was compounded by a troll calling her a 'prostitute' and posting cruel images. When caught, it turned out the troll, a thirty-eight-year-old man, had targeted other bereaved families over the previous four years; he was sentenced to fourteen months' jail.[22]

RIP trolling emerged from a subculture driven first and foremost by the pursuit of 'lulz', the desire to provoke reactions that amuse the troll and their confederates. The ethos of trolling is a sort of aggressive anti-earnestness: nothing is to be taken seriously, even death itself.

But interestingly, as Whitney Phillips found during her ethnographic exploration of troll communities, some RIP trolls justify their actions by insisting that what goes on online is not 'real' grief:

> As I found, the vast majority of trolls' RIP energies were directed at these 'grief tourists', users who had no real-life connection to the victim and who, according to the trolls, could not possibly be in mourning. As far as these trolls were concerned, grief tourists were shrill, disingenuous, and, unlike grieving friends and families, wholly deserving targets. The much-ridiculed statement 'I didn't know you but I'm very sorry you're dead' was therefore seen as a declaration of trollability.[23]

What connects all of these disparate modern phenomena – complaints about funeral selfies, the willingness to joke about death in the case of 'Gregg Jevin', grief-policing and RIP trolling – is a generalized anxiety over the *realness* of the online world. This attitude was already in evidence even in the pre-Facebook era, when technology scholar danah boyd was researching the early social network Friendster: 'In discussing Fakesters, Batty was quick to point out that there's no such thing as an authentic performance on Friendster – "*None* of this is real."'[24]

Fake deaths

'Fakesters' were Friendster users who, for a variety of reasons, pretended to be someone they were not. Just as not everyone was who they said they were, not all deaths were what they appeared to be, either. If you were on the blogging platform LiveJournal in the early 2000s you probably saw a few cases like this: a user would set up a new LiveJournal account, and spend some time posting about their life.

Perhaps the life they narrated was an intriguing one, full of especially lurid details – or maybe not. But then the user would describe how ill they were becoming, followed by an announcement of a devastating diagnosis. Their followers would rally around their ailing friend. Sympathetic comments would flood in. Treatments would be attempted but come to nothing. The user would report getting sicker and sicker, until – silence. After a delay, a new post would appear, claiming to be a partner or family member, passing on the awful news that the user had passed away. A fledgling online community would be plunged into a new kind of grief, mourning a person they'd never met yet felt gutted to lose.

Then the user, still very much alive, would register another account with a different name and do the whole thing all over again. This happened often enough that a LiveJournal community, fake_lj_deaths, sprung up to investigate and expose the epidemic of fake deaths.

These people weren't simply frauds. They were lying, but it was a different category of lie from people like 'wellness' blogger Belle Gibson, who 'cured' herself of brain cancer with a special diet and health regimen and made hundreds of thousands of dollars selling her story and lifestyle, before it emerged she'd never had cancer at all.[25] The LiveJournal death-fakers didn't seem to make money from what they were doing. Their behaviour had psychological rather than materialistic roots.

Posts to fake_lj_deaths petered out and finally stopped in 2012. But the LiveJournal death fakers weren't the first people to feign illness or death on the internet, and nor would they be the last. *Wired* journalist Howard Swains found numerous cases between 2007 and 2009, including a knitting forum contributor who 'faked her death rather than provide patterns she had been commissioned to design'.[26] More recently, a troll named Eris provided a gripping and strangely moving fable of the internet era. 'Eris' had built up both fierce friendships and deep resentment among players of the game Epic Mafia. Eris took his handle from the Greek goddess of chaos, and he lived up to the name. He uncovered and published personal details of other players ('doxing'), used his programming skills to change the outcome of games and mess with site moderation, and set up traps to link people to obscene imagery. Yet despite making life chaotic and even unsafe for Epic Mafia players, their community was shocked and anguished when he posted a suicide note. Googling his real name brought up an obituary showing he had, indeed, died and been cremated.

In fact, Eris had set up not just the obituary but the entire news website on which it was hosted. 'I really hadn't wanted to be myself for some time, but it's rather impossible to cease being yourself in real life', he later told journalist Alina Simone. Some Epic Mafia players were planning to dox Eris to stop him returning to the game; 'I figured I'd just beat them to the punch and dox myself via fake suicide'. What Eris hadn't foreseen was how much grief his 'death' would provoke, or how guilty that would make him feel. That's why he confessed, and brought himself back to life.[27]

Not all cases of online 'pseudocide' involve such clear rationales. The range of behaviours here runs from a trend of children bluntly asking for 'likes' on social media because, they claim, their pet or parent had died,[28] through to full-blown cases of what's been unofficially called 'Munchausen by Internet'.[29] In Munchausen syndrome (now properly known as factitious disorder imposed on self), the patient feigns illness, while someone with Munchausen syndrome by proxy (factitious disorder imposed on another) makes a person in their care sick (or appear to be sick). In the case of Munchausen by Internet, the patient takes advantage of the ability to pretend to be someone else online to perform illnesses they aren't actually experiencing, or invents a sick child or other family member as a proxy. Someone with 'regular' Munchausen syndrome faces the challenge that they must continue to stay 'sick'. An actually dead person cannot experience the sympathy of those who mourn them. A Munchausen by Internet patient who 'dies' online, however, sidesteps both these inconveniences.

I'm not a psychologist, so I don't intend to explore the question of what motivates online death-fakers. Instead, let's take a moment to consider what all this means for the people taken in by them. When we grieve for a death-faker, who are we grieving for?

This is a philosophical question rather than a psychological one. It's not about the strength of our feelings, nor is it about how healthy or reasonable those feelings are: we'd feel pretty much the same whether the person really had died or had (unknown to us) faked their death. It looks like there are three options to describe what's going on when we are struck by grief for an online death-faker:

1. We don't experience grief, but something else that feels indistinguishable from grief.
2. We experience real grief for a fictitious person.
3. We experience real grief for a real person, but our knowledge of that person (including their current death-status) is radically incorrect.

Which of these options we choose here will depend very much on our theory of personal identity – are the persons we encounter online *real* or not?[30] – and our theory of what it is to grieve. That's a problem because, as Michael Cholbi has recently noted,[31] there's remarkably little written on the nature of grief in the philosophical literature. The answer we give to this question will also have implications for other questions in online ethics. Consider people who have been 'catfished', drawn into a romantic relationship with a person pretending to be someone else:[32] are they really in love, and if so, *who* are they in love with?

All three answers seem to generate problems. To say that what we feel isn't *real* grief suggests that the 'realness' of grief somehow depends on the status of its object, not what it feels like to grieve that object. Subjectively, real grief and faux-grief would feel the same. That makes the difference between real grief and faux-grief dependent on something totally extrinsic to the person who grieves. It would be like saying someone never really loved a partner who, over decades, only pretended to love them back.

Could real grief, then, be directed at a fictional person? On that view, I am genuinely grieving, but no actual person corresponds to the object of my grief. The problem is that love, and the grief that attends it, arises in engagement, in what Martin Buber called 'the lightning and counter-lightning of encounter'.[33] When I grieve a death-faker, there really *was* another party involved, another actual consciousness I engaged with, even if they don't answer to the description of the person I'm now mourning. It takes two to tango, even if one of the partners is feigning all the steps.

Yet it also seems wrong to say that I'm genuinely grieving someone but that I just don't realize that the person I'm mourning is totally different to how I believe them to be. You can certainly grieve for someone who you think is dead but is in fact alive. That is what happened in the case of Eris – but while Eris didn't use his real name online, he wasn't pretending to be a different person, either. Can you grieve for someone who is both alive *and* has a completely different identity from the one you thought they did? That's quite different from the experience of grieving for someone who then turns out to be alive: the death-faker generally doesn't, so to speak, come back from the dead in quite the same way. In 2013, American college football player Manti Te'o led Notre Dame to an upset 20-3 victory just days after both his beloved grandmother and his girlfriend Lennay had died. But when journalists looked a little closer it turned out that Lennay, who Te'o had never met in person, did not in fact exist; Te'o had been catfished by a man who he understood to be Lennay's cousin.[34] Was Te'o never really in love, actually in love with (and mourning for) a woman who never existed, or unknowingly in love with a living third party? None of these answers are convincing on their face, and all, for the reasons outlined above, run into difficulty fairly quickly.

No clear answer presents itself here. That, in itself, is telling. We come back again and again in this book to a sense of the ambiguity of the dead online, who are both gone and still with us. That ambiguity, as we'll see, tracks a deep fissure in our very being.

But there's another thread that runs through our discussion so far. We started this chapter looking at real deaths and how they became somehow less real through the internet. We then looked at contested forms of online grief, fake deaths and mourning for people who never died or never existed at all. Haunting all this is a generalized suspicion that the internet, and the people we meet on it, is somehow less than fully real. So before we can explore the ethics of internet immortality, we need to do some metaphysics. If we are to decide whether people can survive death through the internet, we need to work out if the things on our screens are even people at all.

2
Online identity

Let's restate the driving question of this book: do we survive death via the internet?

Phrased so baldly, that seems like a preposterous question with an embarrassingly obvious answer: No, we don't. The dead are dead regardless of what they leave behind online, whether that's a shoebox full of old letters or a social media profile. You don't call off a funeral because the dear departed forgot to delete their old MySpace account.

There's something obviously true in that. As we'll see in later chapters, there's a real risk that digital technologies will lull us into forgetting the destructive force of death, shielding us from accepting what's been lost when someone dies. Yet while the dead are no more, they are not *simply* no more; they aren't non-existent in the way that, say, unicorns or square circles are non-existent. 'Talk of the dead', as Palle Yourgrau puts it, 'is of an entirely different order from, say, talk of the tooth fairy'.[1]

The Roman philosopher Lucretius notoriously claimed that there's no difference between non-existence before birth and non-existence after death – and so given we don't fear the time when we didn't exist before we were born, it is irrational to fear death.[2] Against this, Charles Hartshorne insisted there is indeed a difference, and a critical one at that: before I was born, 'there was once no such individual as myself, even as something that was "going to exist." But centuries after my death, there will have been that individual which I am. This is creation, with no corresponding de-creation'.[3] George Washington doesn't exist now. He didn't exist before he was born, either. But he didn't exist in a *different* way before he was born to the way he doesn't exist now. Before he was born, nobody could speak of George Washington at all; now, even though he has been dead for over two centuries, you know exactly who I'm talking about and can probably even picture him from paintings. Yourgrau, though working with a very different metaphysics than Hartshorne, concurs that the dead are 'a set of nonexistents easier to grasp than the unborn. We can name specific dead people and we know many detailed facts about them, whereas it is difficult to find a single unborn whom we can isolate and refer to with a name.'[4]

In that difference, according to Hartshorne, lies the key to immortality: the fact that the dead *have* lived can't be taken away from them. Once we have become real, we attain a reality that even death can't take away from us. As soon as we are written into the 'book of life', we cannot be erased *from the book* even if our 'character' is long dead in the later chapters. From where we're up to in the book, Washington died a few hundred pages ago, but the pages that feature him are all still there. For Hartshorne, though, this isn't enough. A Book of Life needs a reader. And we humans are pretty poor readers: we only ever know a fraction of what goes on in the minds and lives of others. The secrets of Washington's heart were only a little less hidden from those who lived alongside him as they are for us. For Hartshorne, then, our immortality requires a reader who reads *everything*: 'In short, our adequate immortality can only be God's omniscience of us.'[5]

Unlike Hartshorne, I don't hope for – or fear – a divine reader. But I do want to agree that the persistence of the dead is real, in an important (if tragically incomplete) way. This ambiguous existence is one the philosophy of death has struggled to accommodate, or has simply denied. Yet it refuses to be dissolved.

But we're getting ahead of ourselves. As we saw in our discussion of dying online, there is a major worry that threatens to scuttle any notion of digital immortality before we even begin: the worry that our online presence isn't real. If what we are online isn't really *us*, then any hope for a digital afterlife is doomed. So this chapter, and much of the next one, are something of a preparatory detour: before we can consider whether and how the dead could survive online, we first need to get clear about what we are online.

Second Life

We'll begin by considering a part of the internet that's already well past its prime. Second Life is an online environment ('virtual world') created by San Francisco-based Linden Labs in 2003. In 2010 there were around 20 million registered users of the site[6]; by 2017 the number of active users was reckoned to be under one million.[7] Users create an avatar (whose appearance they can customize) to move around the Second Life world and interact with objects and other users. Second Life has its own economy, with a few users even becoming rich in real-world currency through their in-world economic activity. Second Life arguably never quite lived up to the hype around it, but it did flourish long enough to confront researchers with a number of unsettling questions.

Foremost among these is: what is the ontological status of this computer-generated world – that is, is it *real*, and real in what ways, and with what consequences? The answer might seem to be partly given in the name itself. As sociologist Margaret Gibson notes, 'The very name *Second Life* provokes the question of ordering categories – a first and a second life and by extension a first and a second death.'[8] A second life is almost certainly going to be a *secondary* life, a parasitic life that cannot exist without a 'real' life as its host, though it would be very wrong to assume that this means a second life is superficial or shallow.[9] Second Life residents do in fact distinguish between their 'real' and 'second' lives in this way, and generally 'the flesh and bone world of embodied existence in the sensuous life world of human attachments will always take precedence'.[10]

Yet even if a second life is derivative of real life, avatars are not mere toys or masks. Rather, says Gibson, the way Second Life residents mourn their dead in particular demonstrates how the avatar 'partakes of *personhood status* with some level of material and emotional gravitas embodied in this life form and corporeal image'.[11]

So Second Life unavoidably raises the question of what the relationship is between people and their avatars: one of identity, or something else? This is precisely the question the philosopher Marya Schechtman takes up. After all, for at least some people, 'virtual worlds are not mere fantasies or fictions but are instead a genuine part of their lives, involving experiences and actions as real as any others', a fact which, for philosophers interested in the problem of personal identity, cries out for explanation.[12]

Schechtman's question is whether a Second Life user is merely role-playing as their avatar, like the relationship between an actor and their character, or whether user and avatar are more closely united than this. We're familiar with online avatars mostly from gaming, and few of us would say that we're merely *acting* a particular role with an in-game avatar. I don't *act out* a role in a game; I *take on* a role and *act through it*. (This rather hazy formulation, I hasten to add, is mine, not Schechtman's.) Both King Lear and the protagonist of a first-person shooter game are fictional characters trying to navigate their world successfully, but the player has power to change the outcome while the actor playing Lear does not.

But as Schechtman notes, Second Life differs from ordinary games in having 'relatively few constraints on player identity and activity and no well-defined goals or rules and so (arguably) more closely approximate[s] life offline'.[13] Games have a clear teleology: a purpose or goal towards which all of our actions should be directed. Fail to act in the right ways, and the game is over, or at least fails to advance. In online environments like Second Life, however, there are no such game mechanics. Instead, we find ourselves thrown into a world that's already underway, which we didn't create and have limited control over, with no defined purpose or plan. Sound familiar?

The philosophical problem of personal identity is often cast as the question of what, if anything, makes someone the same person at different points in time. Schechtman is known for developing a particularly influential version of the 'narrative' approach to personal identity (you can also find versions of this approach in philosophers as different as Alasdair MacIntyre and Paul Ricoeur), which sees persons as held together across time by our capacity to tell a story, a life-narrative that unifies events at different times into moments in the life of a single 'character'.[14] While I have reservations about the narrative approach – specifically, I don't think narrative identity is the *whole* story about personhood[15] – there is something right about it too. Feeling responsibility for things I did in the past, or worrying about whether I will suffer in future for the choices I make today, depends in part on being able to tell a story that connects past, present, and future versions of 'me' in the right sort of way. Is there such a story according to which a Second Life avatar can be *me*?

The stories we tell in Second Life may seem quite insulated from our offline lives. My avatar might well have a different name, gender, race, occupation and even a completely different personality.[16] It's tempting to say that even if my online avatar is radically different from my offline persona, it still expresses something of who I am offline, because even if I try to be someone else, all I can ultimately do is provide *my* interpretation of what I think that other person is like. (Hence an actor might still bring something of themselves to a role that's as distant as possible to who they 'really' are.) But let's allow, for the sake of argument, that it's possible to maintain an online persona that's totally different from who I unselfconsciously am in everyday life.

Even then, and even in an online world as different as Second Life, there are a number of ways in which my online and offline narratives will intersect and influence each other. Schechtman gives a range of examples, from trivial ones like avatars becoming unresponsive while their 'owner' attends to real-world tasks to dramatic ones like online affairs leading to real-world divorce. What these examples show is that even if the avatar and the real-life persona are drastically different, they still feature in the same story in a way that assigns both to the main character, so to speak. Schechtman gives us the analogy of a businessman who every so often, and with his wife's blessing, leaves his family at home and heads to Las Vegas for a weekend with his friends. Las Vegas becomes a whole other life, one blissfully detached from his workaday life and responsibilities. Like Second Life, Vegas may seem like a self-contained, separate realm: *what happens in Vegas, stays in Vegas*. But in fact, the boundaries between the businessman's domestic life and his Vegas life are likely to be far more porous than that. If his wife rings while he's at the craps table he'll interrupt what he's doing to take the call. He knows he can spend a bit more money than he would at home, but not so much as to jeopardize paying the mortgage that month. His wife is happy enough for him to cut loose with his buddies, but not to have affairs or casual sex with strangers.

What the Vegas analogy demonstrates, I think, is not just that real-life and online narratives are interrelated in the ways Schechtman describes, but also the deeper fact that we can never wholly leave our moral embodiment at the door when we move from one world to another. Schechtman's reveller doesn't stop being a married father and employee when he touches down in Nevada, just as his bar tab at Caesar's doesn't become someone else's problem when he returns home. There's a larger narrative in which the one individual is sometimes partying in Las Vegas and sometimes parenting at home. What doesn't change across that narrative is that he is a moral agent responsible for the character of his life *including* the decision to go to Vegas and what he does while he's there.

But notice that we can make that claim without asserting that one environment is 'real' and the other is not. Vegas might indeed involve a great deal of pretence and illusion, but that's not primarily what makes going there a problem. Likewise, an ethicist might judge that it's wrong for me to run around shooting people in a virtual game world, or they might instead declare that it's perfectly fine; but whether it's ok or not might not solely depend on the fact that I'm 'really' sitting on a couch rather than slaughtering other beings in a fantasy world. There may be other reasons to worry about what we do online. Say I turn on my game console and fire up the latest instalment in the *Big Steal Car* series, where succeeding in the game requires me to murder people (or at least, murdering people helps me advance in the game faster). It's clear that I do not commit actual murder; nobody is going to jail for playing the game successfully. Yet by playing such a game, perhaps I *am* participating in and perpetuating structures of ideology and power that fuel certain forms of real-world violence (particularly gendered violence). Even where no other actual people are directly involved in what I do in-world, participating in a game-world that endorses certain behaviours might be morally problematic, as Sebastian Ostritsch has recently argued.[17] A universe set up to reward you for gratuitous killing or sadistic torture might be one you simply shouldn't spend time in, let alone pay for. I'm not saying that's true – just that the fact that it *might* be shows that our moral lives don't stop where skin meets joystick.

Likewise, I may not commit actual adultery in Second Life, but in engaging in sexual behaviour with the avatar of another person perhaps I am being unfaithful to my real-life partner in a significant sense.[18] As J. David Velleman has noted, our relation to our online avatars is so close that saying 'I did an action with my avatar' would sounds as odd as saying 'I did an action with my body.' An avatar may be a fictional body, but it's *my* body nonetheless.[19] Avatar sex may not be as real as bodily sex, but it's not as unreal as a mere erotic daydream either. (People laughed at Jimmy Carter for confessing that he'd 'committed adultery in my heart many times',[20] whereas if someone confessed to engaging in extramarital cybersex their remorse would not be nearly so mockable.) As we'll see shortly, this not-as-real-as-physical-but-still-real status is essential to understanding online presence. Binary thinking in terms of real/unreal no longer does the work in these domains that we expect it to, if, indeed, it ever did.

Nearly two decades of research on Second Life has shown that sometimes, at least, a second life isn't something parasitic on a first life, but is rather just a secondary part of one person's life. As Velleman puts it, 'Two distinct creatures, one wholly real and one partly fictional, can be literally animated by one and the same mind, for which they help to constitute different selves.'[21] The things we do in environments like Second Life *can* be, as Schechtman says, 'subplots in the more comprehensive narrative of the resident, a person who lives sometimes in [real life] and sometimes in [Second Life]. Both sets of adventures are part of the same life because, although distinguishable sub-narratives, they impact each other along the most fundamental dimensions of narrative interaction'.[22] These online environments may be very different from our everyday life, yet they are environments where *we* choose to go, and where *we* decide what we do. That means we can't simply offload moral responsibility for what happens there.

This point goes much further than environments like Second Life, too. It generalizes across our everyday experience of online communication. Indeed, as Gibson notes, part of the appeal of Second Life today is the capacity to live not just double, but *triple* lives: residents can evade not just their 'real life' identity but can also detach from 'the network sociality of a digital first life'.[23] Their avatar can be a (notionally) different person from who the user is in physical space *and* who they are on social media. That fact only makes sense because of one of the most surprising changes of the twenty-first century so far: the increasing dissolution of the distinction between online and offline.

After cyberspace

My first encounter with the internet was in 1996, as a first-year university student. Every few days or so I'd go to a computer lab on campus to check my email via Telnet. I remember someone leaning over one day, pointing to the university homepage on her screen, and asking me 'how you get to the wider internet'. I don't think I knew how to answer. We both had a vaguely spatialized understanding of the internet as a *place*, but no idea how you got there.

When the internet first came into public consciousness, it quickly gave rise to the idea of 'cyberspace', imagined as an ontologically separate realm to the one we normally inhabit ('meatspace', a term which, thankfully, never caught on in the same way). Here was a whole other world that could be accessed through a desktop computer – a place where law, morality and even physics didn't necessarily apply. The word 'cyberspace' was coined long before the internet, by artists Susanne Ussing and Carsten Hoff, though its contemporary meaning arguably derives from William Gibson's 1984 novel *Neuromancer*, where he glosses it as 'a consensual hallucination'.[24] Popular depictions of computers as portals to other worlds in movies and TV had long prepared the ground for the idea of cyberspace; perhaps that's why it survived while other early metaphors for the internet, such as the 'information superhighway', did not. Movies like the *Matrix* series continued to bolster the idea of a separate computer-generated reality even as they played on existing anxieties about what was real and what was mere simulacrum.

Cyberspace was never much more than a metaphor: it was in fact always a material place, made of wires and circuits and glass. But then, hallucinations (even collective ones) are ultimately material too, events in the squishy matter of the human nervous system. In many ways the metaphor was quite self-serving. Conceptualizing 'cyberspace' as a place apart let us pretend it was somehow outside of our real life, a sort of electronic Vegas – except, as we've just seen, even Vegas isn't really Vegas in that sense. Those entering cyberspace did so from meatspace, where their bodies remained, and where they remained ethically answerable for what they did the whole time. (And, as many people discovered to their cost, legally answerable as well.) The online/offline barrier was always leakier than it might first have seemed.

As early as 1999 commentators started to see the cyberspace metaphor fraying at the edges, as the internet increasingly permeated the 'real' world.[25] The distinction between the online and offline worlds started to break down in earnest as soon as 'cyberspace' was no longer somewhere you had to physically seat yourself at a computer to visit (and then wait for the 56k dialup modem to make its comfortingly physical boing-boing-hiss noises as it connected). The increasing ubiquity of the internet in work and leisure, followed by the rise of smart phones and wearables, meant that 'cyberspace' was no longer a separate place we visited but part of the fabric of our economic and social universe. Where once I had to go to a special room and sit on a terminal just to check my emails, now I can be simultaneously talking to the person physically in front of me while we each scroll through options for where to go for dinner nearby, while surreptitiously taking part in arguments on Twitter at the same time. We no longer visit cyberspace. Now we move through space that is always partly cybernetic.

In 2013 a group of scholars released a document called *The Onlife Manifesto*. The authors of the manifesto claim that information and communication technologies (ICTs) are changing our world in ways that make our existing concepts inadequate to grasp and control reality. New technologies upend old assumptions about the relation between nature and humanity, individual persons and responsibility, citizens and political power, and the public and the private. Accordingly, ICTs pose enormous tasks for thought, tasks that, we might add, have already begun to get away from us.

The manifesto is intriguing, if short. What is most interesting for present purposes is the choice of the term 'onlife', a neologism coined by one of the authors, Luciano Floridi, to refer to 'the new experience of a hyperconnected reality within which it is no longer sensible to ask whether one may be online or offline'.[26] Are you online or offline right now? Are you sitting at a computer? No? But do you have your phone nearby; will you check it if it buzzes or dings? Am I online right now? Yes, in that I'm on a networked computer with any number of distractions threatening to overwhelm my focus on writing these words. But I'm not 'online' in the sense in which I would have used the term in the late 1990s on a platform like ICQ chat: to be 'online' then was to be *directing your attention to the internet*, not to writing a book. To 'be online' was also to be available to chat with others. (You could also set your account to 'appear offline', which only reinforces that 'online' was as much an other-facing status as an individual state.) But then even when writing this book I *do* frequently direct my attention to 'the internet', sometimes even to dig out references for what I'm writing. And when I get up to make myself a coffee, I'll take my phone with me, probably so I can continue yet another unproductive Twitter argument without interruption. You can see, then, why a term like 'onlife' might appeal. It captures the way in which the online/offline binary no longer maps easily, if at all, onto the way in which ICTs permeate our lifeworld.

You might well worry that this is generalizing from one relatively small, privileged part of the global population, and you'd be right. We might also insist that talk of a 'collapse' between the online and offline worlds has been over-hyped. There are still plenty of things we can only do face-to-face or on paper, and you can still – if only just – disengage completely from electronic communication. Even so, we are fairly close to the point at which disentangling the online and the offline will be moot.

Yet even if we want to dig in and defend the online/offline distinction, the things that made cyberspace so alluring – its disembodiment, its disconnection from our everyday identities, and its lack of consequences – have been steadily decaying for well over a decade. We may or may not be fully 'onlife' (and no disrespect to Floridi and colleagues but I doubt that term is going to take off any more than 'meatspace' did), but we're certainly enmeshed in online networks in far more pervasive, and more surprising, ways than the old language would suggest. The remaining residents of Second Life might still enjoy the illusion of shifting between lives and worlds, but for the rest of us, there is increasingly just *one* world.

Anchored identities

There's a famous New Yorker cartoon by Peter Steiner in which two dogs are sitting in front of a desktop computer. 'On the internet', one says, 'nobody knows you're a dog'. You may know the cartoon, but you might not realize it was first published in July 1993, at a time when the internet was only just beginning to enter homes and businesses. Yet the joke embodies a worry that's still very much with us: that the people we encounter online aren't *real*, or rather, that it's not *really them*.

There are certainly many places online where you can be a dog (or more likely a bot)[27] without anyone knowing. Twitter, for instance, is full of bot accounts, as well as accounts that are anonymous, parodies of real people, or that are operated wholly in-character. (A personal favourite is @KimKierkegaardashian, an account which mashes up the tweets of media personality Kim Kardashian and philosopher Søren Kierkegaard, to brilliant effect.) The pseudonymity of the platform can be a very good thing. Most importantly, it allows people in marginal, vulnerable or sensitive positions to comment publicly. Anonymity can however also facilitate abuse, often of those same marginalized users. Nor is anonymity reliable, as users are sometimes outed or even doxed, such that their online personas become publicly linked to the person behind them. Interestingly, when this happens some people seem to adopt something like the 'telic possibility' stance discussed in the introduction: when the identity of Twitter maestro 'wint' (@dril) was uncovered, many Twitter users simply refused to look. They just preferred not to know who wint 'really' was.

Twitter is a somewhat uneasy hybrid of public and private. Many accounts reveal little or nothing about the people operating them, and many others are the organ of businesses, organizations or brands rather than named individuals. Not all social media environments are like this, however. Social networks such as Facebook involve what have been called *nonymous* online identities: that is, the real names of the participants are known to other users, even if those names are not actually used for reasons of privacy or preference. Indeed, Facebook founder Mark Zuckerberg explicitly saw the unification of online identities as not merely desirable, but ethically demanded:

> 'You have one identity,' he says emphatically three times in a single minute during a 2009 interview. [...] 'The days of you having a different image for your work friends or co-workers and for the other people you know are probably coming to an end pretty quickly,' he says. He makes several arguments. 'Having two identities for yourself is an example of a lack of integrity,' Zuckerberg says moralistically. But he also makes a case he sees as pragmatic – that 'the level of transparency the world has now won't support having two identities for a person'.[28]

There are other, decidedly less noble concerns at play here of course. As José van Dijck notes, platform providers have strong commercial reasons for 'promoting the online self as a standardized tradable product'.[29] It's easier to gather data on your behaviour and preferences – data that can then be used to target you with advertising – if there's only one 'you' to assign that data to. If you're running separate online identities for your vegan activism and BDSM escapades, it will be harder for faux-leather whip makers to find you.

We're quite used to nonymous environments. In fact we spend much of our lives in them, from kindergarten to the workplace through to the retirement home. Sites like Facebook largely extend existing relationships that originate in or are connected to these spaces. (I do have Facebook 'friends' I've never met, but I know who they are because we've interacted in other ways, or we're mutual friends with people I know from offline contexts.) So in at least some social networks, users stand in relationships that are 'anchored' via offline friendships, institutional affiliations, mutual acquaintances and so on.[30] That puts limits on the sort of identity claims users can make. It's much harder to pretend to be someone completely different to who I am face-to-face. Not impossible, of course: Facebook is still full of 'sock' accounts (from 'sock puppet', i.e. a fake cover identity used online for specific purposes) as well as scammers and frauds. But this is understood as a deviant, somewhat illicit use of the medium; people who unknowingly interact in good faith with sock accounts can rightly still feel aggrieved. As Whitney Phillips notes in her exploration of online trolling, the idea that impersonation violates community expectations goes right back to the earliest days of the internet:

> Not only were these trolls a threat to the utopian dream of early cyberspace, they gestured to the norms against which their behaviors were said to transgress – namely that 'true' identities do not deceive, that any form of deception undermines community formation, and even more basically, that pure communication is naturally and necessarily preferable to some inauthentic alternative.[31]

More surprisingly, in addition to being anchored to existing relationships, social network users are also increasingly anchored to their bodies as well. This may seem counterintuitive. Where once it was straightforwardly true that, as Erika Pearson put it, internet users were 'disembodied and electronically re-embodied through signs they choose to represent themselves',[32] social networks increasingly started to call into question the assumption that 'cyberspace' was incorporeal.[33] Users found it harder and harder to get away from their bodies. In an earlier epoch of social media, there were the infamous 'MySpace Angles', a misogynistic policing of (mostly) women's profile pictures for using supposedly flattering camera angles. Then came photo tagging, then *automated* photo tagging where a social media network identifies your face from other photos already on the platform – the system *knows what you look like*. Add to this the geotagging of photos and posts and the collection of biological data from health apps and wearables, and it becomes clear just how linked your body is to your social media presence.[34] Every time you tell your fitness app to share on Facebook that you've just completed a workout, you are embodying yourself more and more online. Emojis and reaction gifs are likewise used, as the linguist Gretchen McCulloch notes, as representations of the user's body and how it is responding to the conversation in real time.[35]

These forms of online embodiment have already started to encompass death, in poignant ways. In April 2017, dozens of people were watching an interactive map of cyclists competing in Australia's 5,500 km Indian Pacific Wheel Race when they noticed Mike Hall's dot had suddenly stopped moving. As social media reports of a fatal accident in that area came through, the community of self-professed dot-watchers shared a sickening realization: Hall, in second place and closing in on the finish line in Sydney, had been hit by a car and killed.[36] Online embodiment can be a source of comfort in the face of loss, too. In 2012, Randy Pristas casually mentioned to his daughter Andrea that he'd waved at a Google Street View car as it drove past his house, photographing the street for use in Google Maps. When Randy died five years later, Andrea went to Google Maps to check, and sure enough, there was her dead father, his face pixelated out for privacy, waving to Google's cameras and, unknowingly, to those he left behind.[37]

In their work on Second Life, Margaret Gibson and Clarissa Carden develop the notion of 'digital flesh', the sort of embodiment we develop over time through immersion in digital spaces. Flesh is, they note, vulnerable, something mortal and capable of being harmed. Not everyone who has an avatar in a virtual world automatically has digital flesh: it's something that has to be built up, through 'the development over time of connections, of memories, and of temporal and emotional investments'. Only through that sort of engagement do you create something that can be hurt, 'through processes of engagement which render them necessarily vulnerable to moral harm'.[38] Gibson and Carden call this a metaphor. What I want to suggest as we move through this book is that 'digital flesh' is more than just a metaphor, even if it is less than literal.

Too good to be true

The worry people have about the reality of internet interaction isn't just that the people we meet online might be frauds or catfishers or bots or dogs. It's that even sincere people don't present their *real* selves online. It's reasonable to assume that even with the increased tethering of our bodily and online selves, the identities we construct and manage in our social networks will still contain a degree of exaggeration and distortion; 'Certainly', note Dean Cocking and Jeroen van den Hoven wryly, 'on social media hardly anyone is dull or boring'.[39] But that's scarcely a new development. The technology researcher and commentator danah boyd once argued that as all online profiles are essentially performative, with users trying to present a particular view of themselves, *all* profiles are necessarily less than authentic.[40]

But if 'authentic' here simply means 'free from attempts to present a particular view of oneself' then it's unclear if any social behaviour, online *or* offline, could count as authentic. We're always putting our best foot forward, so to speak. Authenticity is a deeply contested philosophical concept, and we are a long way from an agreed definition of what the term even means or exactly why it matters.[41]

Making things worse, there's a tension between how we ordinarily use the term and how philosophers use it. We often speak of authenticity as if it is being true to some 'real' inner self – a use that philosophers of authenticity like Heidegger would be utterly allergic to. For Heidegger, authenticity is not about being true to some pre-existing core identity, but about not living in a thoughtless way, simply doing 'the done thing' as determined by other people.

Yet we all recognize, or think we recognize, online inauthenticity when we see it. We open Instagram and see the latest 'influencer', all languid smiles and spotless white couches or sipping branded smoothies on tropical beaches with improbable zest, each post trailed by a dozen or more hashtags. For most of us this sets off our bullshit detectors – and I here mean 'bullshit' in the technical sense offered by Harry Frankfurt: the liar knows the truth and cares enough about it to try to hide it from you, whereas the bullshitter doesn't particularly care whether what they say is true or not, just so long as you believe what they tell you.[42]

It's the cleanliness that gives it away. Every social media persona is curated to a certain extent, just as we curate our identities in everyday interaction too. With the sort of influencers we're talking about here, however, their online lives are *too* obviously curated for us to take them seriously. They may not draw attention to how monetized the whole exercise is, yet they reek of commerce. One of the conditions that narrative identity theorists have stipulated for narratives to hold us together across time is that the stories we tell about ourselves must not merely be *coherent*, they also have to be *true*. What that means, in part, is that other people would agree with the story that the agent tells about themselves, and that no *better*, more accurate narrative is available.[43]

The influencer, presenting their Insta-perfect life to their devoted followers, leaves out a great deal in the way they narrate their life, but that's not necessarily a problem in itself. Every story necessarily cuts out a vast amount of detail in order to be intelligible; a story that included every trivial and irrelevant detail would not, in fact, be a story at all. Rather, the problem with the influencer's online presentation of their life is that it leaves out too much that fits into another, more accurate story of who they are. They're scrubbed of the lapses that serve in part to make us who we are: our frustrations, our failures, our pettiness and sleaze.

We're not all influencers, of course, but we do all arguably engage in some degree of identity management in our social media lives. To use the terms famously coined by the sociologist Erving Goffman in the late 1950s,[44] social network users attempt to *give* a presentation of the self through language or gesture, rather than involuntarily *giving off* a picture of what we're like.[45] Shenyang Zhao and colleagues found that what Facebook users presented to the world 'were the hoped-for possible identities users would like to, but have not yet been able to, establish in the offline world'.[46] Yet that too is not as far removed from offline identity practices as we might think: *practical* identity, the set of practical and emotional commitments we tacitly or explicitly endorse, usually involves an aspirational element, some sense of what Stanley Cavell called our 'next self'.[47] Our online personae may well be an uneasy blend of who we are and who we wish we were – but in that, they're no more inauthentic than how we present ourselves the rest of the time.

Still, we now have new and more powerful tools with which to sculpt and present our identities to the world. Brand management has moved from the realm of a tiny number of famous people to the realm of the everyday user. Each of us now has a persona to sell in the social marketplace. As van Dijck points out, in part this is people simply doing what they've done for a very long time: modelling themselves on celebrities, but with new rewards (clicks, likes, retweets), as well as new pressures.[48] We are of course constrained by context. You wouldn't, say, go describing intimate details of your love life or family arguments on LinkedIn, a space where you're meant to put forward a professional, teflon-coated presentation of who you are to colleagues and potential employers. But then, you wouldn't do those things in the boardroom either. (You might find a private space at work to gossip with or complain to your co-workers – and you can do that in LinkedIn too.) We arguably self-censor on any social media platform, but the ways in which we do so differ more in degree than kind from how we self-censor in social and work situations, and are often linked to precisely the same offline relationships too.

We're also constrained, perhaps far more seriously, by the mechanics of the specific platform. In Facebook, for instance, the rich spectrum of interpersonal relationships gets shoehorned into the artificial binary friend/not friend,[49] while tastes and interests are similarly presented under preset categories.[50] Your ability to respond to someone else's content is likewise channelled into certain set forms. Where once you could only 'like' a status, post or comment on Facebook, now you can click a button to declare yourself sad, angry, surprised, or amused – but you still can't 'dislike' it. (That of course also impacts on how you can mourn the dead online too.)[51] And of course, unlike in the world of synchronous, face-to-face or audio-visual conversation, you are subject to terms of service including community standards and can have your words – and you yourself – removed if you break the rules. Offline, we sometimes run up against difficulties in describing our relationships to others without awkwardness, and we find ourselves picking from a predetermined menu of acceptable phrases and responses far more often than we might think. Even so, these platform-based constraints are real, and it's worth considering what sort of commercial, social, and political imperatives have shaped them. It's also worth noting the ways in which internet users manage to circumvent them.

It's also important to note that we do not create our online identities alone. Social media identities are made up of material sedimented in place by other users as well as yourself. The photos that present you online are posted not just by you, but by 'friends' and 'friends of friends'. The content of your timeline will be not just your own words but those of others, both posting directly to you, posting elsewhere and tagging you in, and commenting and replying to comments. The self that emerges is very much a group creation. But once again, we don't create our offline identities alone, either. Other people bestow names, family histories, nationalities, religions and cultural identities on us, often before we're even out of the womb.[52] Others continually situate us, promote us, relegate us and tell us (and make us) who we are. Alasdair MacIntyre offers the classic summation: 'we are never more (and sometimes less) than the co-authors of our own narratives. Only in fantasy do we live what story we please'.[53]

So, here's what we've seen so far. In reply to the worry that our online profiles are not 'us', we've seen that the boundaries between the offline and online are now far more volatile, while the firewall between who we are online and offline has also become less tenable. We've also seen that social network users create an online identity that is anchored in their offline relationships (however tenuous these connections might be), tied to their bodies and linked to a self-conception that is reflective and aspirational. If that identity is inauthentic, constricted, or full of pretensions to greatness, it is probably no more so than how we live our identities offline in any case. Or if it *is* worse, this is a matter of degree. One key objection to the idea of living after death via our online identities – the objection that it is not really us online in the first place – has now been cleared away.

Crucially, though, social media sites aren't just a place where we build a version of ourselves. They're also a place where we communicate with others. They are, as we'll now see, part of our face. And that will have startling implications for what happens when we die, but leave our face behind.

3

Presence

The self we're each constructing online is, as we've just seen, increasingly anchored to our 'real world' personas. This is even true of online fantasy worlds to some extent, but it is particularly true for social media. For all its opportunities for self-aggrandisement, sanitized self-presentation and outright fraud, the self that we show the world on social media is nonetheless real in much the same way as the self we present 'in the flesh' is real. In fact, our online selves are increasingly fleshy.

In this chapter, I want to shift slightly to talk about the phenomenology of how we encounter others online: that is, what it is to experience 'meeting' other people through social media. A medium is something through which information is transmitted, and thus something that *gets in between* us and the person sending us the information. Part of the reason people view online communication as less than fully 'real' is precisely this in-between factor, the sense that the medium creates a barrier to direct, real human contact, that it distorts what it transmits. We're sometimes told that mediation is why people abuse other people so much more online: the largely text-based format obscures the person behind the words, making it drastically easier to say things we would never say to someone 'in person'.

It's true that some online platforms require us, if we aren't to turn into trolls or abusers ourselves, to work hard at reminding ourselves that there is a real person on the other end of our invective. Moreover, when a medium amplifies things out of their proper proportion, the scale of that communication can itself create harm. Consider the phenomenon of internet 'pile-ons', in which someone is berated by a huge number of users all at once for something they've said or done. Each individual criticism might well be justified, and lots of people repeating the same criticism many times doesn't amount to a *stronger* criticism: if you tell a lie, and four hundred people call you a liar for doing so, that doesn't imply you're as bad as someone who has told four hundred lies. Yet the sheer volume of critical comments can itself become abusive *even if* every individual act of criticism is reasonable and legitimate by itself. Interestingly, this phenomenon appears as early as the mass media of the nineteenth century, as the Danish philosopher Søren Kierkegaard noted in 1848:

> For example, by telling in print of a young girl (giving the full name – and this telling is, of course, the truth) that she has bought a new dress (and this is assumed to be true), and by repeating this a few times, the girl can be made miserable for her whole life. And one single person can bring this about in five minutes, and why? Because the press (the daily press) is a disproportionate medium of communication. Suppose someone invented an instrument, a convenient little talking tube which could be heard over the whole land – I wonder if the police would not forbid it, fearing that the whole country would become mentally deranged if it were used. In the same way, to be sure, guns are prohibited.[1]

We now have a global, always-on talking tube; you can make up your own mind about the derangement.[2]

Yet what I want to suggest in this chapter is that in our online lives, we overcome the alienating effects of mediation far more than we might think. Something we get from in-the-flesh engagement is definitely missing when we meet each other through screens. Yet telepresence is still a form of *presence*. Even through screens we get a sense of who the person is, of their distinctive way of being in the world – in short, their *phenomenality*, the what-they're-like-ness of that person. That, I want to argue, means we really are, in some more-than-metaphorical sense, present with those we engage with online.

I'm writing these words during the global COVID-19 pandemic, at a moment of worldwide death and disruption, when millions of people are confined to our homes and video calling services such as Zoom and Skype have suddenly replaced face-to-face work and social contact. My children are contemplating virtual birthday parties and playdates. The phenomenology of telepresence, its adequacy and limits, is suddenly a daily, lived issue, as people try to remain in each other's lives. Many people are learning new ways to be present with the absent. And as we'll see, the phenomenological success of telepresence also has the startling implication that we are in fact in the presence of the dead, in some more-than-metaphorical way, when we engage with their online traces.

But focussing on how we experience other people online, and how others experience us in turn, draws our attention to a fundamental divide. How we exist for *others* may in fact be very different to how we exist *for ourselves* – and that in turn has crucial implications for online survival. Death, and the ways in which we survive it, splits us right down the middle.

Ghost photography

The dead have always appeared to us in memory and in dreams. And we have always used technology to help the dead persist. The Romans wore ritual masks bearing the likenesses of their ancestors as a way of keeping the distinctive appearance of the dead, what they were *like*, in the world. (Today, you can store your loved one's ashes in a custom urn in the shape and likeness of their head – or, if you prefer, the head of a celebrity.)[3] Portraiture has preserved the appearance of the dead for as long as humans have been able to draw; the increasing sophistication of art is in some ways a technology of embalming. Whilst portraits preserved the dead as they were while alive, however, they could only ever be as good as the artist who made them. The artist is a medium in both senses of that word: that through which information travels, and someone who connects the living with the dead. In so doing, something of the artist no doubt infects the presentation. Angolo Bronzino's portraits of sixteenth-century Florentine nobles transfix you with their startling, penetrating gazes, so much that you feel yourself forcefully confronted by their long-dead subjects. Yet all such portraits are, unmistakably, Bronzino. They are somehow suffused both with the piercing otherness of the individual sitter *and* with their creator and mediator.

Wax or plaster death masks, on the other hand, took the artist out of the equation. (Though death masks were for a very long time made solely to serve as models for portraits and sculpture.) Yet the cost of dispensing with the mediation of the artist was that the likeness of the dead could only be captured *after* death. The restful, beatific faces we see in death masks are deeply uncanny. They show us a likeness that has already retreated into non-being. Much like standing next to a corpse, they give us a sense both of being present with the dead and of having just missed them. (Unless, that is, we don't even recognize a death mask for what it is: if you've ever done first aid training you've probably performed mouth-to-mouth resuscitation on 'L'Inconnue de la Seine', an unknown young woman supposed to have drowned in the 1880s and whose alleged death mask provides the prototype for the first-aid mannequin 'Resusci Anne'.)[4] Something similar applies to the late Victorian practice of corpse photography. A sepia image of a family posing with a newly dead child or adult at once captures both the presence and the absence of the dead relative to the rest of the family.

Of all our technologies for preserving the dead, portrait photography has been especially powerful. As Margaret Gibson notes, photography allows the long-dead to figure in the lives of the living even when photographs predate living memory, and even when the photos are poorly executed.[5] The Frankfurt School theorist Walter Benjamin famously denounced the way in which mechanical reproduction robs art-objects of what he called their 'aura': the glow of authenticity that attends historical artefacts, the sense of genuine 'presence in time and space, its unique existence at the place where it happens to be'.[6] The aura of *the* Mona Lisa that you experienced while standing in the Louvre is missing from the poster of the Mona Lisa you bought in the gift shop on the way out, no matter how well printed it is. Yet Benjamin, curiously, makes an exception for portrait photography:

> The cult of remembrance of loved ones, absent or dead, offers a last refuge for the cult value of the picture. For the last time the aura emanates from the early photographs in the fleeting expression of a human face. This is what constitutes their melancholy, incomparable beauty.[7]

Roland Barthes, in his remarkable meditation on photography known in English as *Camera Lucida*, goes one step further than Benjamin. Barthes discusses Alexander Gardner's striking photograph of Lewis Powell (also known as Paine), one of John Wilkes Booth's co-conspirators and the attempted assassin of Secretary of State William Seward, in manacles and awaiting his trial and execution. Like those Bronzino portraits, the photo is uncomfortably present. Powell stares directly at – into? – the viewer with a look that largely defies description but cannot be evaded. Barthes notes that the image is suffused with our foreknowledge that Powell *is going* to die *and has already* died.[8] He claims that every photo is a presentiment of death in this way. But every photo is also a testimony that the dead *have been*. For Barthes, a photograph preserves a very distinctive ontological relation to its subject. It is not merely a 'representation' but an 'emanation' from the person and the past, and thereby a 'certificate of presence' that cannot be denied.[9]

Yet while Benjamin was prepared to concede that portrait photographs retain the aura of the person depicted, he denied that the same was true of film. Photos retain some sense of what was unique and distinctive about a person, but, according to Benjamin, this aura is lost in front of the film camera. Why, though? Film, after all, is a photographic medium, and one that reproduces so many aspects of the person, from gait to tone of voice, which still photography cannot.

I suspect that Benjamin's claim that auras persist in still photography but not in moving film has less to do with the intrinsic material properties of these two media and more to do with the way in which technologies become transparent to us as we incorporate them into our embodied experience. To see why, let's look at a remarkable short story that's meant as a warning about the limits of electronic communication – but which accidentally points to just how real telepresence can in fact be.

The Machine Stops

In 1909, the novelist E.M. Forster published a science fiction story entitled *The Machine Stops*. The story is set in a future where the surface of the Earth has become uninhabitable, with humans now living in subterranean buildings. There, people sit alone in their rooms and share 'ideas' with people all over the world via an electronic network called 'The Machine', which offers what we would now think of as video and audio communication. You can see already why it's sometimes claimed, perhaps a little too quickly, that Forster anticipated the internet. At the very least, the world he sketches is in some ways uncomfortably familiar.

In this world, it is still possible to travel to see other people face-to-face, but this has become uncommon. A young man, Kuno, nonetheless asks his mother Vashti to come visit him. Vashti, who lives on the other side of the world, dislikes airship travel, and in any case doesn't see why she should need to visit Kuno at all given she can see him through the Machine. Kuno tries to explain to her why he longs instead for direct, non-mediated contact:

> I see something like you in this plate, but I do not see you. I hear something like you through this telephone, but I do not hear you. That is why I want you to come. Pay me a visit, so that we can meet face to face, and talk about the hopes that are in my mind.[10]

Hubert Dreyfus cites 'The Machine Stops' as neatly summing up the problem with 'telepresence', the sort of presence we can have to each other through electronic communication.[11] Telepresence is an increasingly common term in the corporate and public service worlds where it's used to describe meetings where particularly high-fidelity videoconferencing is used. Interestingly for present purposes telepresence has even started to appear in the very conservative context of the funeral industry: 'CARL', a mobile robot equipped with a screen, microphone and speaker, can attend funerals on your behalf, allowing 'you' to move around the room and talk to your fellow mourners via Skype.[12] Yet despite telepresence being everywhere, there's remarkably little agreement in the academic literature on what telepresence actually is, or how it even relates to the concept of 'presence' more broadly.[13] In his work on self-presentation which we touched on earlier, Erving Goffman speaks of presence as *co*-presence, a situation in which people are located with each other in such a way that they 'sense that they are close enough to be perceived in whatever they are doing, including their experiencing of others, and close enough to be perceived in this sensing of being perceived'.[14] While nobody since has been quite able to agree on whether telepresence is a property of the medium itself or the participant, or whether it is a matter of perception or feeling, the thread that runs from Goffman through to Dreyfus is the idea that a sense of *being there* is a sense of *being with*. Telepresence, at least in the sense relevant for our purposes,[15] is about the sort of connection we normally have in the direct physical presence of another, with all that entails: mutual visibility, vulnerability and unavoidability.

Dreyfus, quite reasonably, sees Forster's story as a warning about the dangers of disembodied communication. The Machine's users experience the world at second-hand and deal only with abstract, fetishized ideas instead of concrete things or people. (At one point, Vashti is scandalized when an airship crew member reaches out her hand to stop Vashti falling over, the practice of bodily contact having become obsolete.) Kuno, who has seen the surface of the earth for himself and is trying to maintain experiential connection with it, seeks the sort of direct human contact with his mother that the logic of the Machine actively works to frustrate.

Forster's warnings are indeed worth heeding. (In particular, people eventually forget that the Machine is a human construction and come to deify it, casting out the 'unmechanical' unbelievers. Their faith ultimately prevents them from noticing that the Machine is breaking down.) For Dreyfus, the problem with telepresence is due to the lack of embodiment, and specifically to the absence of that mutual vulnerability that comes from sharing physical space with another person.[16] As we saw in the last chapter, the internet is perhaps not as completely disembodied as Dreyfus assumed, and nor are we anywhere near as invulnerable as he'd have us believe.[17] Kuno finds the form of telepresence available to him inadequate, yet even then it is not entirely disembodied: he hears the timbre of his mother's voice across the telephone line, an echo of the construction of her vocal chords.

We mustn't deny that there is something missing in virtual communication, as the families of prisoners denied in-person visits in favour of video calls can attest.[18] But deficient communication is not the same thing as no communication at all, and while telepresence may lack much of what we get by physically being there with someone, it's not the same as simple absence either. A phone call is not as good as a hug, but it's clearly not as bad as no contact whatsoever. And it is far from obvious that, despite what Forster and Dreyfus say, it's a mere simulacrum of presence either.

For while Forster's story is uncannily prescient, there's something to learn from the ways in which 'The Machine Stops' *doesn't* ring true for us, too. Consider Kuno's declaration that 'I hear something like you through this telephone.' A century on, the phrasing jars: I don't hear something *like you* in my phone, I just *hear you*. It's true that what comes out of the phone is an electronic reconstruction of the voice of the person on the other end. But we don't notice this, both because the reconstruction is so lifelike that we take it to simply *be* life, and because unlike Forster we've grown up with telephony as an embedded part of our way of existing. This form of telepresence has become second nature to us. Practically and emotionally, it's *your voice* that I hear. It's *you* I talk to.

That way of putting things sounds suspiciously like what Luciano Floridi has called the 'epistemic failure' model of telepresence.[19] On this view, telepresence happens when we fail to notice the machinery of mediation. We feel ourselves to be co-present with the person we're talking to until something goes wrong with the technology to remind us we're not. Floridi is critical of this idea, resting as it does on an assumption that whenever we achieve telepresence we've made a sort of conceptual mistake, wrongly believing that we're hearing someone else's voice instead of a mere reproduction. But we could look at things another way. Instead of saying I've merely forgotten that your voice is mediated, I've come to *see through* the mediation.

Twentieth-century phenomenologists noted the ways in which tools get taken up into our embodied experience such that we come to act and see through them. Maurice Merleau-Ponty, for instance, famously argued that a visually impaired person's cane 'has ceased to be an object for him, it is no longer perceived for itself; rather, the cane's furthest point is transformed into a sensitive zone, it increases the scope and the radius of the act of touching and has become analogous to a gaze'.[20] The cane feels the world and is transparent for its user in the same way as our bodies are transparent for us most of the time as we touch and move things. You feel with your fingers, but you don't *feel* your fingers themselves unless they start to ache. Likewise, the internet and the platforms we use on it can disappear for us as our attention focuses instead on the people they bring through to us, without this being a sort of grand mistake or act of forgetfulness.

There may be, as the phenomenologist of technology Don Ihde has argued, an element of 'technofantasy' in all this, a desire to have the good things technology offers while also enjoying the spontaneous transparency of the ordinary lived body as if the technology wasn't in fact there.[21] Yet we really do, I think, achieve a degree of embodied co-presence with others where the technology slides into the background. The reason Kuno's phrasing sounds odd to us today isn't that in the intervening hundred years we've tacitly forgotten how phones work, so much as that we're not distracted by the mechanics of telephony. The phone or the screen falls away and *you* come through.

Social media presence

While Kuno's description of the telephone sounds wrong to us, it might ring considerably truer when we turn our attention to social media. Could we say 'I see something that looks like you on this Facebook profile, but I do not see you'? At first blush, it seems we could indeed.

For one thing, we might want to claim that social media just isn't as experientially rich as most of what we'd normally think of as telepresence. Hearing your mother's voice down a telephone line and seeing her in a video 'plate', even if Kuno found it lacking, seems more like being in her presence than reading her tweets or checking out her Instagram posts. Even in Forster's story, the Machine engages more than one of our senses at once. Ihde notes that early 'monosensory' media technologies often used exaggeration to compensate: think of those over-the-top facial expressions and gestures of the silent movie era.[22] For Ihde, those of us living early in the twenty-first century are quite accustomed to audio-visual media, but are still a long way from a virtual reality experience that's just as multisensory as ordinary embodied experience. We can watch movies, but we still can't touch or smell them.

It seems natural to assume that the more senses a given medium can engage, the more 'real' the experience, and thus the greater the sense of telepresence, it will offer. That 'realness' should also make it easier to avoid miscommunication by giving us access to non-verbal cues like facial expressions or tone of voice. 'Media Richness Theory' (MRT), first put forward in the 1980s,[23] confidently predicted that, all else being equal, people will prefer to use richer forms of communication instead of leaner ones. We ditched the telegram for the telephone, so naturally we'll ditch the telephone for the videophone, right?

Well, no. We often *do* choose the leaner form of communication over the richer. Video calling didn't supplant the voice phone call; the text message, a less rich form of communication, did. It turns out we seek out different media with different affordances for different purposes.[24] Very often, that means preferring something asynchronous (where we don't have to respond immediately like we would face-to-face or on the phone) and more text-based rather than visual and immediate.

Yet communication hasn't become less real than it was in the telephone era. More people than ever can be present in our lives at once; we just have more control over how they are present. We can keep them at the relative distance of a text or email, or let people into the greater intimacy or more sustained attention of a video call. (At the other extreme, we can deliberately block some people from seeing us, however imperfectly.) Something is lost in that, of course. A phone call imposes itself on you in a way that a text or a direct message might not. It demands response, much as having a person directly in front of you demands response simply by being there. Yet we manage to avoid people face-to-face, too. The experience that Emmanuel Levinas described as the 'face' of the other breaking through the crust of our self-contained egoism is something no form of communication can guarantee – not even face-to-face.

No medium can force us to take the face of the other seriously, not even the portrait photography Benjamin was so impressed by. Yet social media can, and often does, capture that Benjaminian aura of the other person. Recall that for Barthes, every photo is an emanation of the person it depicts – even if they're long dead. The image on paper is something that reaches out from the past and confronts us face-to-face. Social media does this in multiple ways, through photos, text, video and audio. In a short space of time it's become one of the primary ways in which people appear to us now, people who once would have only been visible either in person or in episodic memory. Moreover, it is a site where those who appear communicate with us: the face of the other on social media is a face that speaks.

It is also a face that remains, albeit in a more static form, once a social network user has died. Of course, the dead leave many other things behind too, from their corpses to their worldly possessions. Many of these artefacts are suffused with a sense of the dead person for survivors, even when they're only accidentally connected to the person who has died. Your grandfather's watch may have a particular poignancy for you, and while there may be other watches just like it out there, *this* watch belonged to your grandfather. Yet that may not mean anything at all to a watch connoisseur offering to buy it from you. Your social media profile, however, is *essentially* yours in a way your watch is not. It does not acquire its relationship to you in the essentially accidental way that, say, the randomly assigned code name 007 becomes integral to the (fictional) individual James Bond. Instead, social media profiles are *born* as vehicles for identity performance and maintenance. It is built to present you specifically and individually; it gives out your identity as part of its essential construction.

Distributed selfhood

Our question is whether we can survive death online. To begin to answer that, I've gone to some length to say that who we are online *really is* us, and that those we encounter online *really are* other people. But this raises a further, troubling question: *where* are these online people, exactly?

Philosophers of personal identity might insist here that persons are just another type of thing, and things are locatable. Exactly *how* things can be located might vary from thing to thing: Michelangelo's David is a big chunk of carved marble in the Galleria dell'Accedemia in Florence, whereas the CIA is made up of people who are distributed across the world, for instance. Exactly what constitutes the class of things we call 'people' is a hotly-debated topic. Very roughly, some theorists say we're bodies, some say we're minds (or chains of interconnected psychological states), some say we're brains, some say we're organisms, a few still say we're souls, and some say persons don't really exist at all. But one thing all these theories have in common is that they let us pin down where persons are.[25] The pope is in Rome, the US president is in the White House, you're in seat 38B wondering why you ever thought this would be a good book to read on a plane, and so on.

Clearly, the selves we present online aren't like that. If that's *me* on the screen, not just a representation of me, then I can be on any number of screens at the same time as well as on multiple servers in multiple places. Personal identity, you might object, just doesn't work like that. If I ask where a particular Instagram celebrity is, 'on millions of screens around the world' isn't the sort of answer I'm looking for. I'm looking for an answer of the form 'Tahiti' (if I'm wondering where that latest pic of a spectacular sunset was taken) or 'Portland, Oregon' (if I'm asking where the user is usually based).

My claim here is that persons – and I'll have more to say later about a distinction between persons and selves which is doing a lot of the work in this argument – are not so tightly tied to a specific place. Bodies and animals may be located at particular places, but *persons* in this broader sense are indeed distributed. Queen Elizabeth II is currently in Windsor Castle, yet in another sense she is present in all the countries where her face appears on coins and banknotes. Your practical, intersubjective identity is not reducible to your body, or your organism: as a person in this practical identity sense you also exist in the brains of others, in paper and electronic legal documents, and in the various social media profiles through which you make yourself present in the lives of others (and they in yours).

This is of a piece with what Richard Heersmink calls 'distributed selfhood', an extension of the increasingly widespread notion of extended cognition. Minds are distributed, according to extended cognition theorists, in the sense that they are not simply in our heads, but exist in the way in which organisms interact with other things in the environment, including other minds. On this view, when you do some sums on the calculator app on your phone, or check your calendar to jog your memory about how long it's been since a particular meeting was held, the phone or the calendar becomes part of the cognitive system that is your mind. Even outside of extended cognition theory, the idea of prosthetic memory has become well-established: mechanisms through which we offload some of the work of remembering from organic memory to inorganic objects. (Think of all the phone numbers you used to remember by heart, and how few you remember today now that your phone stores them all for you.)

If minds are distributed across the environment in this way, the argument goes, so too are persons. We exist not simply as bodies, nor simply as minds rattling around in skulls, but 'smeared' across the world through all the things we bring into our personhood and through which we are instantiated. As Heersmink puts it, 'The complex web of relations we develop and maintain with other people and artefacts partly constitutes our self, implying that we are essentially a soft self. Personal identity can thus neither be reduced to psychological structures instantiated by the brain nor by biological structures instantiated by our biological organism.'[26] ('Soft self' is a term taken from Andy Clark: 'a constantly negotiable collection of resources easily able to straddle and criss-cross the boundaries between biology and artefact.')[27]

On that model, digital artefacts like social network profiles, being very much part of our extended mind – and as we've seen arguably part of our extended *body*, not least our face – become part of our distributed selfhood. The various places in which we appear online, and the screens and servers and minds that sustain these, all become part of that extended body.

The startling thing is that this extended body is left more or less intact when users die – so intact, in fact, that these digital resources can act as memory prostheses in the stronger sense[28] of allowing those who never even knew the deceased to encounter them. We now live with digital resources that, in the sociologist Ruth McManus' words, both 'reveal the presence of the dead stored and storied in new digital media' and 'stitch the breach that opens up between those who knew the dead person and those who did not; between living memory and tales of ancestors'.[29] To see how, we must now, at last, descend into the digital underworld.

4

Electric corpses

Nearly half a century has passed since the novelist Italo Calvino published *Invisible Cities*, a postmodern re-imagining of the Venetian traveller Marco Polo's discussions with the great Mongol *khagan*, Kublai. Calvino's Polo describes to the emperor the cities within his dominions that Polo has seen. These cities are not real places, but fables. They are cities of language, of rhetoric and concept. Some read like jokes, others like daydreams, still others like nightmares.

One city that lingers with the reader is Eusapia, where the boundaries between the living and the dead have become volatile. (It is perhaps no accident that Eusapia Palladino (1854–1918) was one of Italy's most famous – and outrageously fraudulent – psychic mediums.) Eager to soften the transition into death, the Eusapians have built an underground replica of their city for the dead, tended by an order of hooded monks:

> All corpses, dried in such a way that the skeleton remains sheathed in yellow skin, are carried down there, to continue their former activities. And, of these activities, it is their carefree moments that take first place: most of the corpses are seated around laden tables, or placed in dancing positions, or made to play little trumpets. But all the trades and professions of the living Eusapia are also at work below ground, or at least those that the living performed with more

contentment than irritation: the clockmaker, amid all the stopped clocks of his shop, places his parchment ear against an out-of-tune grandfather's clock; a barber, with dry brush, lathers the cheekbones of an actor learning his role, studying the script with hollow sockets; a girl with a laughing skull milks the carcass of a heifer.

To be sure, many of the living want a fate after death different from their lot in life: the necropolis is crowded with big-game hunters, mezzo-sopranos, bankers, violinists, duchesses, courtesans, generals – more than the living city ever contained.[1]

But something strange began to happen. The monks found that every time they went down into the replica Eusapia, things there had changed slightly. The dead were making small, thoughtful innovations to their city – so many that over time the replica city started to become unrecognizable. And the living Eusapians, not to be outdone, started to copy the changes the dead had made. Until:

They say that this has not just now begun to happen: actually it was the dead who built the upper Eusapia, in the image of their city. They say that in the twin cities there is no longer any way of knowing who is alive and who is dead.[2]

Like every other community, the Eusapians have had to deal with the question of how to dispose of their dead. Bodies are awkward. They take up space, they're heavy, they start to decompose quickly and can spread disease. Some societies have hit upon responses to this problem not too different from that of the Eusapians. Western philosophers tend to view death as something that happens instantaneously, no matter how long the process of dying itself might take. One moment you're alive, the next you're dead, with no in-between.[3] The difference is understood as a sudden biological change, although specifying just *what* that change is turns out to be surprisingly difficult.[4] That assumption that life and death are binary, however, may be driven by intuitions that are far more culturally variable than we assume. The Toraja people of South Sulawesi in Indonesia, for instance, view death as a somewhat more extended process. Torajan dead are spoken of as *to'makula* ('one who has fever' or more broadly 'a sick person') and are not regarded as dead until their funeral rites.[5] That might be months or even years away, during which time the dead are kept embalmed inside the house. Even after they are finally buried, the dead do not disappear physically from the lifeworld. Every August, as part of a festival called ma'nene, they are taken back out of their graves. Bodies are dressed up, walked around, cleaned, perhaps have make-up re-applied and offered lit cigarettes. Many get a change of clothes before being reburied with their grave gifts and items such as their mobile phones.[6] Like the fictional Eusapians, the Torajan dead remain visibly arranged, to some extent, as participants in the world of the living.

The contrast with contemporary death practices in the 'global north' is striking. The most salient feature of the dead in the contemporary West is their *in*visibility, with both the dying and the dead kept out of sight. For the most part the Western dead stay sequestered and invisible, either interred or entombed, or cremated and scattered or held in urns or columbaria. Much of our funerary and memorial systems can be understood as enormous mechanisms for controlling and reducing the visibility of the dead.

Sometimes however, even with the best of intentions, this arrangement doesn't hold. As we'll see in this chapter, one of the (many) unexpected side-effects of the rise of social media is that the dead have become increasingly visible in the spaces of the living. Instead of being safely quarantined in graveyards, the dead are mixed in among the living, present and unchanging. In Chapter 2, we saw that in social media we tend to present a slightly idealized version of ourselves – so many big game hunters and duchesses. In social media, the dead enjoy a static parallel existence in which they are living their best lives, in a place where it's sometimes unclear who is alive and who is dead.

Entirely without meaning to, we've built our very own Eusapia.

Networked ghosts

As we've seen over the last two chapters, we are increasingly present online, so much so that our profiles and avatars are becoming integrated with our flesh as part of what we *are*. Our online presence is not so much a tool we use as an aspect of our *face*, part of how we are present to, seen by, and communicate with the world. Go online and you find yourself face-to-face not just with photographs or lines of text but with other souls, eyes burning with consciousness – what Wittgenstein beautifully called 'the light in the face of others'.[7] But what happens when the source of that light is extinguished – when the users behind these online identities die?

Vibeke[8] was one of the mothers in our antenatal class when we lived in Copenhagen. Once the babies were born the class became an instant mother's group, and sure enough we all ended up friends on Facebook even after many of the new parents had drifted back to our home countries or elsewhere. That was how, eight years after we'd first met her, we heard the horrible news that an aggressive cancer had carried Vibeke off before she'd turned forty.

As I write this, Vibeke's Facebook profile is still online. She is dead, but Facebook doesn't know that. Every morning, Facebook lets me know who among my friends is having a birthday that day. Once a year I get a notification that Vibeke is a year older; yet she is not. On her Facebook 'wall', well-wishers come to wish her a happy birthday 'in heaven'. Then suddenly, jarringly, there'll be a comment that simply says 'Happy Birthday'. No 'in heaven' or other acknowledgement of Vibeke's absence. A friend or acquaintance who has not yet heard the news, perhaps?

This is an afterlife as banal as it is uncanny. And it is happening on a scale we can't even begin to assess.

Nobody quite knows how many dead people there are in any of the major social networks, let alone other online platforms. There were already estimates nearly a decade ago of around thirty million dead Facebook users.[9] That figure would be dramatically higher today, but nobody – not even Facebook – can say just how high. In 2019, Carl Öhman and David Watson attempted to at least work out how many more Facebook users would die in future.[10] On the most conservative model (according to which no new users join Facebook at all), the dead will outnumber the living by mid-century. On a high-growth model, we'll have to wait until the early 2100s for that to happen. Both scenarios, of course, assume that Facebook will continue in some recognizable form – a deeply unsafe assumption, as anyone who had a MySpace account can confirm.

For now, at least, the dead remain a minority on social media. Yet they make their presence felt. Once people started joining social networks in serious numbers, it was inevitable that some of them would die while still active users of the service. The mechanics of these services also meant their profiles would, unless the service intervened, remain visible as if they were still alive.

There was, as social media companies quickly came to realize, no real playbook for this. Even commercial self-interest doesn't give any clear guidance. On the one hand, the dead are good for business. A dead social media user may not be clicking on any ads or generating sellable consumer data themselves, but just by being there they are still providing 'content' for living users to engage with. The profiles of the dead keep your monetizable eyeballs on the site just that little bit longer. As Öhman and Floridi have noted, there's perhaps no more literal demonstration of Marx's concept of 'dead labour'.[11] On the other hand, having the dead so visible can be upsetting for those same living, cash-spending customers. As the digital dead began to pile up, Facebook started getting complaints from distressed users who had received automatically generated messages suggesting they 'reconnect' with their dead loved ones. The dead, just like the living, were also turning up in 'friend suggestions' created by the site's algorithms. (Years later, this problem would reappear when photos of the dead became swept up in Facebook's cheery, algorithmically-generated videos.)[12]

The challenge was how to keep the dead profitably online without disturbing living customers too much. As Facebook's head of security, Max Kelly, put it: 'Obviously, we wanted to be able to model people's relationships on Facebook, but how do you deal with an interaction with someone who is no longer able to log on?'[13] By 2009 this problem had become too big to ignore. The answer was to find a new, half-way status for the digital dead, one that reflected the ambiguous character of the dead themselves: memorialization.

If your loved one dies, you can notify Facebook and request that the profile be put in a memorialized state. (You'll need to provide proof of the death, to stop people from maliciously getting other users' accounts deleted.) Memorialized accounts have words like 'Remembering' or 'In Loving Memory' added to the profile name to signal that the user has died. Nobody can log into a memorialized account, but a dead user's 'legacy contact' – someone they've nominated to act on their behalf after their death – can change the profile picture and write a 'pinned' post explaining the loss. A memorialized account will not appear in friend suggestions. If you're a 'verified immediate family member' you can also request that, instead of memorialization, the account be deleted. If nobody does either of these things, the profile simply sits there unaltered. If a survivor has the password they'll be able to operate the account, though this is generally a violation of the platform's Terms of Service. The user's premortem privacy settings, whatever they were, are maintained. So if you set everything to 'private', locking down your online life to all but your nearest and dearest, it will stay that way – and if you live your life in public, that's where it remains, even after you're gone.

The endless wake

If the dead aren't deleted, the result is something that is at once both familiar and unsettling. Although this phenomenon is historically quite new, we're fortunate that it has already been quite heavily studied in psychology, sociology and media studies.

Online memorials have existed since late last century, often in the form of simple condolence book websites or in more multimedia-driven ways. Even in social media, dedicated online memorials are often still used for public mourning of events, such as mass-casualty events, celebrity deaths or deaths that otherwise attract significant media attention. In these cases, those mourning together will mostly have never met the deceased personally – which, as we've seen, can provoke some extreme negative reactions.

For many people who die, however, there's no need to set up a separate, dedicated mourning page – because the much smaller community of those who knew the dead person already have access to a space in which they can gather virtually to mourn. Everything they need is right there on their deceased loved one's social media profile: photos, 'memories' and fellow mourners who can keep the dead alive in shared recollection. In effect, a profile site (whether memorialized or not) is converted into a tribute site, a space of commemoration in which an impromptu, organic community of grief appears. It's a sort of open-ended electronic wake. Yet there are important differences.

How people act in these environments is, as I say, already quite well-studied.[14] One of the most interesting findings is that mourners writing on Facebook walls, for example, address the dead in the second person. Not 'I wish they were still here', but 'I wish *you* were still here.' While this is not universal, it was noted as early as the MySpace era, and has become more ubiquitous over time.[15] Elaine Kasket notes that whereas in the early 2000s only about 30 per cent of visitors to online memorials spoke in second-person, addressing the dead directly, her study of late-2010s Facebook memorial pages found 77 per cent of mourners doing so.[16]

Nor is this address to the dead a one-off event. People come back again and again, for months and even years, leaving messages on important anniversary dates or just whenever they feel the need to reach out to the person who has died. This aspect of online mourning behaviour is less like a wake and more like what we do at gravesides. But where once you had to go out to the graveyard to speak with the dead, now you can do so on the bus, on the couch, anywhere you find yourself.

This goes beyond social media. Some people continue to send SMS texts to those they've lost. While they are sometimes self-conscious about the fact they're texting the dead, the mobile phone provides the bereaved with a means to maintain a sense of connection and speak *as if* they are heard.[17] In a particularly moving case in 2019, Arkansas woman Chastity Patterson sent a text to her late father's phone number, as she had done every day in the four years since he'd died. This time, though, she got a reply. It wasn't her father who texted her back, but 'Brad', the stranger who had been allocated her father's old phone number. Brad revealed that just as Chastity had lost her father, he had lost a daughter and that the daily updates from Chastity had sustained him through his own grief. Interestingly, Chastity took this response as a moment of closure: 'Today was my sign that everything is okay and I can let him rest!'[18]

Of course, those posting on Facebook walls know that the audience for what they write includes other Facebook users. Yet many users report that they *do* take themselves to be communicating with the dead as well, without necessarily having an idea of how that could be possible.[19] They act as if the departed can genuinely read what they say. Kasket notes that people even apologize to the dead for missing birthdays and the like; 'Facebook is apparently so exclusively effective at facilitating connection that an inability to log on could entirely prevent one from making contact.'[20] Even so, Kathleen Cumiskey and Larissa Hjorth's interviews with bereaved social media users uncovered a great deal of ambivalence about whether the dead could really read or see the things that were being posted and texted to them.[21]

We could write off such practices as simply confused, or superstitious, or perhaps just a by-product of our evolved 'offline social reasoning' capacity, which lets us think about and plan interactions with absent others – which may also explain why everyday afterlife beliefs tend to focus on the survival of others first and ourselves second.[22] More charitably we might think back to the Wind Phone that we met in the introduction, and see these practices as a sort of make-believe, using the affordances of an existing means of communication as if the dead were still listening at the other end.

It's particularly easy to imagine the dead are listening because they're still where we left them, seemingly unaltered, in the place where we would speak to them before they died. We saw above that social media provides a remarkably rich way in which we are *present* in each other's lives. When we die, that presence stays as it was, at least in the short term and often for much longer. The dead remain as visible as they were before, to the same people who could see them before, and in the same place where until recently they spoke and acted. The online identity created when the user was alive stays in place, unchanged, but also unnaturally unchanging. The dead continue to show their face to the world, yet that face has become unresponsive. Our Eusapia, like Calvino's, is a place of uneasy but compelling continuity.

As Kasket notes,[23] this continuity between premortem and posthumous appearance sets social media profiles quite apart from other kinds of online memorials. Some people find this powerful sense of continuity distressing. That, after all, is why Facebook introduced memorialization, so that users wouldn't be confronted by the dead while going about their regular online lives. Yet that online presence can very often be a profound comfort to the bereaved too. Ben Ranaudo, a private in the Australian Army, was killed during operations north of Tarin Kot in Afghanistan in July 2009. His Facebook page quickly became a space of commemoration. A year later his sister Amy told journalists that 'It's brought him back to life a little bit, you can hear him laughing. It's something no one would have expected to happen. It's a way of immortalizing him.'[24]

Just as in Calvino's Eusapia, too, the once-sequestered dead are increasingly mixed up among the living. Social media, as Michael Arnold and colleagues put it, brings the dead out of 'institutional spaces, such as mortuaries, funeral homes, or cemeteries' and celebrates a repositioning of the dead very much within the everyday flow of daily life'.[25] Your dead Facebook friends sit alongside your live ones. As in Eusapia, it can sometimes be hard to know on social media who is living and who is not, as Vibeke's unwitting well-wishers show. Without the cues that pick out memorialized profiles (such as 'in loving memory' or 'remembering' added to their name), and the sort of messages people tend to leave on them, you could very easily look at such a profile and not realize the person has died. In those cases, we can end up interacting with someone who, we might say, is actually not there. Or do we? And are those who *knowingly* text the dead or leave messages on their Facebook walls merely play-acting, taking part in a sort of spiritualist ritual, or something else?

As you might have guessed, I think there's more going on here than mere play-acting. To say that *either* people really think they're talking to the dead *or* they're just pretending is a false dichotomy. There is a third, altogether more unstable but true-to-our-experience option: we really do talk to the dead *and* the dead really are no more. We're already familiar with that existential ambiguity of the dead from our pre-digital lives. In fact, the paradox of the dead, their both being and not-being at the same time, is something we've known as long as there have been corpses.

Digital remains

In our discussion of Second Life, we encountered Gibson and Carden's illuminating concept of 'digital flesh'.[26] We've also seen that online life is drastically more embodied than is sometimes supposed. So: does 'the way of all flesh' also befall this digital flesh? Do we leave behind digital corpses?

Indeed, 'digital remains' is not infrequently used as a label for the things we leave behind online.[27] At first blush, that may look like a cute piece of academic hyperbole. We do sometimes speak of, say, the 'literary remains' of a dead author. Yet whereas we strongly disapprove of grave vandalism, we don't accuse someone who scribbles notes in their copy of *The Great Gatsby* of 'desecrating' Fitzgerald's literary remains. We owe a very different kind of regard for dead bodies than we do letters and documents – even in the case of the very-long-dead, as we see in controversies over repatriating human remains from museums and universities to the indigenous communities from which they were taken. Corpses matter to us in a very particular way.

When we try to say *why* corpses matter, though, we run into trouble. Most, though not all, philosophers of death accept what Fred Feldman called the 'termination thesis', the claim that persons cease to exist at the moment of biological death.[28] One moment you're there, the next you're gone, leaving only a corpse that's not *you*. If that's the case, then it's hard to see why we care about corpses at all. Some corpses may have value for organ donation, and more broadly corpses might be thought to have 'sentimental' (for want of a better word) value for families.[29] Yet the care with which we treat corpses goes well beyond making sure these forms of value are protected. Aristotle notes that 'We also throw away useless body parts and ultimately our body, when it is dead; for the corpse is useless. On the other hand, those who have a use for the dead body preserve it, as in Egypt.'[30] And yet, neither the Greeks nor we moderns regard corpses in such a ruthlessly pragmatic way: we treat them with a degree of reverence that implies the same sort of intrinsic dignity as live persons. We don't treat corpses reverentially *despite* the fact they are essentially refuse; rather we dispose of corpses *despite* the reverential regard in which we hold them. (It's interesting to consider: would we bury or cremate corpses if they didn't decompose at all? Would our norms around corpse disposal just be about space management?)

In *The Dominion of the Dead*, Robert Pogue Harrison claims that every culture responds to a certain 'charisma' of the corpse,[31] which demands that we treat it with a certain care:

> The corpse is the site of something that has disappeared, that has forsaken the sphere of presence, that has passed from the body into … into what? Death? The past? Another dimension? We hear those words and understand them abstractly, but faced with the spectacle of a dead body the primitive mind did not

think to itself: 'My mother has passed away into the dimension of the has-been.' It is more likely it thought to itself (something like): 'Here is my mother lying before me. I can see her, touch her, feel her, yet she is not here. How can this be?' How indeed? Only something as resistant as the insensate body of a loved one – the enigma of its expired life and remnant thinghood – could give the anthropomorphic mind its first access to what we abstractly call death, and with it to the ethos of finitude.[32]

That 'remnant thinghood', the sense of being-yet-no-longer-being, radically changes how we treat corpses compared to other classes of object. We could say this is simply extending a courtesy to corpses out of regard for the no-longer-existent persons with which they are obliquely associated, like taking extra care with a book because it once belonged to your late grandma. But I don't think such borrowed prestige can be the whole story. As Raimond Gaita has suggested, we cannot help but see outrages to corpses as being outrages to the deceased, not just to the living who might be offended by it. When Charlie Chaplin's body was dug up and held for ransom, that was a terrible thing to do *to Charlie Chaplin*, even though Charlie Chaplin no longer existed.[33] To say 'of course it's not really a bad thing for him, but for his survivors' already requires a certain reflective move out of the world of moral experience. Within that everyday world, we can understand that those survivors just wanted Charlie Chaplin back so they could bury him – a sentence that only becomes bewildering, or even nonsensical, when we begin to philosophize with it. When it comes to our attitudes towards the dead, as Palle Yourgrau puts it, 'Our hearts here see more clearly than our heads, for these natural attitudes are disturbed by a beleaguering metaphysical conscience.'[34]

Philosophers since Thomas Nagel's landmark 1970 paper 'Death' have worked up arguments to undergird our intuitions about the respect we owe the dead and their bodies, and indeed the fact we have any moral regard for the dead – keeping promises, refraining from slander, and so on – at all. Even the unsentimental Aristotle found the idea that the dead are not harmed or benefitted by what happens to their descendants 'too heartless a doctrine, and contrary to accepted beliefs'.[35] Thanks to all this effort, there are a number of more-or-less standard arguments available now to those who want to answer how the dead can be harmed or benefitted and yet not exist.[36] These arguments are quite ingenious, and it's well worth taking the time to engage with them. But for present purposes, I don't propose to do so. Nor do I want to offer an error theory of why we revere corpses: I don't want to claim that we treat corpses as if they're the person when *in fact* the person is gone. My point is a phenomenological one: on the level on which we encounter other people, corpses both *are and are not* the person whose body they are. Their uncanniness comes from that contradiction.

That contradiction can also be described in terms of continuity and discontinuity. While we live, our bodies are our key 'substantial realizers', in something like the way that a lump of marble is the substantial realizer of Michelangelo's 'David'. They're what our phenomenal presence, our 'aura' to use Benjamin's term once again, turns up in. When we die, our bodies continue to emit that aura, at least for a time. Our literal face remains, yet the light of consciousness has gone out of it. In Ibsen's play 'The Wild Duck', Doctor Relling cynically declares that while 'Most people become noble when they're standing in sorrow next to a corpse', by the time the grass has grown over the grave that nobility will have deserted them.[37] The presence of the corpse compels us, as no mere assemblage of biological waste could, precisely because of this duplex sense of radical absence and ongoing presence.

This is why 'digital remains' deserves to be treated as more than a mere metaphor or analogy. We've seen that we live increasingly in digital flesh. When we die, the digital bodies we leave behind continue to present our face, embalmed not chemically but electrically. To put things in pre-digital terms, digital remains are more like what's in the coffin than the condolence book at the front of the funeral parlour.

Not everyone buys this, of course. Bernie Hogan and Anabel Quan-Haase, for instance, have objected that when a social network user dies, 'the illusion that submitter and content are one' is exposed.[38] If the profile continues to exist after the person has gone, that just shows that the profile was always more of a curated exhibition *about* the user rather than the user themselves. As we've already seen, this misses just how much our online personas *are* us rather than being representations of or about us. But looked at another way, the gap that troubles Hogan and Quan-Haase here is just another way of describing the old, familiar ambiguity of the dead. You might just as well say that the persistence of corpses dispels 'the illusion that person and body are one'. On the level on which we live, corpses both *are* and *are not* the dead.

Corpses have to be buried, however. They cannot dwell among us, even among the Torajans and the fictional Eusapians. Harrison argues that this disposal is necessary to separate the image of the dead from their body, 'to dispose of the corpse so as to *liberate* the person from its tenacious embrace [...] the dead must be detached from their remains so that their images may find their place in the afterlife of the imagination'.[39] This is true of biological corpses – but what of digital ones? Here, the image *is* the corpse. Harrison, echoing Barthes, notes that the portrait is 'essentially mortuary', a descendent of the death mask.[40] Digital remains are composed precisely of such images, a face composed of a series of words and pictures and sounds, mute but resilient. As we'll see in the next chapter, this drastically complicates how we should deal with these electric corpses – whether we're obliged to keep them digitally embalmed no matter what the cost, and whether deleting them would be a kind of murder.

Survival ...

To speak of 'murdering' a digital corpse may sound doubly ridiculous. A social media profile is not a corpse, and you cannot murder a corpse in any case. I've hopefully made you at least unsure about the first part of that objection, and I'll return to the second in the next chapter. Either way though, up to this point it sounds like the internet doesn't allow us to survive death, except in whatever minimal sense we might be said to 'survive' as a dead body.[41] This is hardly the immortality that Messianic cyber-optimists have promised us.

A prominent American film producer is said to have quipped:

> I don't want to achieve immortality through my work; I want to achieve immortality through not dying. I don't want to live on in the hearts of my countrymen; I want to live on in my apartment.[42]

Nothing spoils a joke like explaining why it's funny, but here goes: the humour here lies in the disconnect between what we *want* from immortality and what we can *have* from the forms of immortality available to us. Suppose that I do, improbably, live on in the hearts of my compatriots through the works I leave behind – from my own point of view, so what? I can experience life in my apartment; I cannot experience other people's memory of me.

It's helpful here to consider what we're actually afraid of when we fear death, and so what we want to avoid. Philosophers have identified at least three distinct kinds of fear of death. Kathy Behrendt points out that there's a certain fear of brute nonexistence *as such*.[43] (Call that the 'zeroeth' type of fear of death.) Mark Johnston notes two different and more specific ways in which we fear death. Firstly, we may worry about all the things that wouldn't happen because of my death. If I drop dead right now, who will finish this book, or raise my children, or feed my goldfish? But secondly, and perhaps more fundamentally, I can fear the loss of subjective experience. As David Lewis once put it, 'I find that what I mostly want in wanting survival is that my mental life should flow on. My present experiences, thoughts, beliefs, desires, and traits of character should have appropriate future successors'.[44] More precisely, what I want is that the mental life I have *now* should flow on such that what turns up in the future, so to speak, is the same mental life as *this* one. What Johnston calls my 'arena of presence and action', the 'place' in which my experience is happening right now, will cease to exist.[45] It's fairly easy, unless you're some sort of raging narcissist, to imagine a world that no longer has you in it; it's much harder to imagine *your* world, your perspective, no longer existing.

Tom Stoppard has his version of Shakespeare's Rosencrantz wrestle with this problem:

> Do you ever think of yourself as actually *dead*, lying in a box with a lid on it? [...] It's silly to be depressed by it. I mean, one thinks of it like being alive in a box, one keeps forgetting to take into account that fact that one is *dead* ... which should make a difference ... shouldn't it? I mean, you'd never *know* you were in a box, would you? It would be just like being *asleep* in a box. Not that I'd like to sleep in a box, mind you, not without any air – you'd wake up dead, for a start and then where would you be? Apart from inside a box. That's the bit I don't like, frankly. That's why I don't think of it ...[46]

Rosencrantz can imagine himself in a box vividly enough. He just can't imagine that there's *nothing it's like* to be in that box, or that he won't wake up. It's that thought of total, permanent *subjective* nonexistence that's so hard to come to terms with. I can leave a will and try to head off some of the problems that drive the first type of fear of death – say, by leaving an endowment to feed my goldfish in perpetuity – but the second way of fearing death is much harder to quash unless you believe in a conscious afterlife. The comfort that lies in the Epicurean thought that if I'm dead I won't care anyway just doesn't tend to stick, as Rosencrantz's horror of waking up in a box demonstrates.[47]

You may notice that I framed both of Johnston's two kinds of death here in first-personal terms: *I'm* afraid *I* may not be around to feed the goldfish, *I'm* afraid *my* arena of presence won't exist. You can easily recast the first kind of fear of death in third-personal terms; for instance, 'If the fish-feeder dies, the goldfish will starve' is true whether it's the fish-feeder themselves speaking or someone else. The second kind of fear of death, however, is irreducibly first-personal. The *me* who will die, the 'arena of presence and action', isn't something other people can access.

These two fears point to a deep division between, to borrow Johnston's terms, the 'person' and the 'self'. I've developed this distinction more technically elsewhere,[48] but here a brief example may help to explain it: when someone stands up to give my eulogy ('it was around that time that he got his first goldfish'), it is the *person* they're talking about: an intersubjectively accessible being, with a name, a location, and a set of familial and social affiliations and liabilities (what Marya Schechtman has called being located in 'person space')[49] and a temporal duration (e.g. 'John Smith, 1812–1882'). As you'll recall from the previous chapters though, the idea that persons have one specifiable physical location becomes considerably wobblier once we consider the ways in which we're present in electronic networks.

Selves, in our technical sense, are something a bit different to persons. They're always first-personal, and always present-tense. Others can know you as a person even better than you do ('I don't think you realise just how much you over-use examples about goldfish'), but nobody else has access to your self, by definition. Your perspective on the world is irreducibly and inescapably yours. To survive as a self requires that you continue to have experiences; without such content, there is no perspective. That's why the quip about immortality in one's apartment makes comic sense. What's it like to live on in your work and the hearts of your countrymen? Nothing: there is *nothing it is like* to live on as a book or a memory. There is nothing it is like to be a corpse, either, even in Eusapia; many of the subterranean residents of Calvino's city lead more exciting lives than they did on the surface, but they feel no excitement, nor even awareness. For themselves, they are nothing, for there is no 'them' for them to be for. You can see how Rosencrantz gets so tied up in knots.

Yet as we've seen, corpses remain, in an ambiguous way, persons – for others. The person dwells amongst us, as a body, as a memory – things that may seem insubstantial and yet which can continue to exert profound influence over people's lives. Regardless of which arguments we use to make our experience of the dead metaphysically respectable, they remain with us as what philosophers sometimes call 'moral patients': the people to whom we owe duties, including duties of love and remembrance. This is absolutely not to deny that the dead live on in a radically diminished way; otherwise the sense of radical loss would make no sense. But there is still a phenomenal sense in which, for us if not for the dead themselves, their moral identity extends beyond the boundaries of their biological lives. Selves may not persist in the lifeworld, but persons do.[50]

Our online lives, as we've seen, disperse us across time and space in newly enhanced ways. Specifically, it disperses us as *persons*. The version of you that exists on, say, Facebook is intersubjective: it exists partly in, and is largely shaped by, its interactions with others. You sit within a nexus of friendship, family, educational and employment relationships – a social network, no less – and your actions are public to some lesser or greater degree. This online persona can bear at least some degree of your practical identity after you die. Like your corpse it will continue to present your face; unlike your corpse, however, your electronic face won't break down, and it is not limited to how you appeared at one time only. (Many people have photos of themselves on their social media that go back well before social media came into existence.) Your face, your words, your voice all linger, all making it easier for people to remember you and thereby keep you alive as *you*, as a distinct, loveable being, in the experience of the living. It's at best a paradoxical survival, for you both persist and are completely gone all at once. And yet – you persist.

... and non-survival

Still, *I want to live on in my apartment.* The 'you' that survives on social media is a person, or perhaps some fraction or fragment of a person. More accurately, you survive as a dead person in the memory and experience of the living, which you do in a number of places including your grave, your body, your works (of whatever sort) and your online presence. That might help soothe some of your first-type fear of death. Your loved ones will still have the online 'you' to look at, to talk to, to reminisce about. It's surely better than dying and having all record of you wiped out.

As immortality goes, however, we might think this is pretty slim pickings. Kevin O'Neill, in his philosophical exploration of the internet afterlife, concludes fairly quickly that living on via online memorials and digital remains is not the survival he's looking for.[51] The problem is that, as the second type of fear of death shows us, we care about having future experiences. If you had to choose, would you prefer to slip into a state of total and irreversible unconsciousness followed months later by death, or to simply drop dead? I suspect most of us would be indifferent, or maybe prefer instant death so as not to burden our survivors. Total and permanent unconsciousness is, from a first-person perspective, no better than dying. If there's no experience to be had in being a social media profile – and there isn't – this form of ongoing existence fails to capture a big part of what we care about in survival.

The question we set out to ask was, does the internet allow us to survive our death? At the outset, the obvious answer was 'no'. Now it seems we've arrived at an answer that's hardly any more thrilling: 'perhaps a little bit, for other people, but not in a way that we could look forward to'.

In fact, that's a more surprising, and hopeful, answer than we might think. We're accustomed to thinking of death in binary terms. Either you're dead, or you're alive. 'More dead than alive' is still alive and not dead. It might be difficult to declare sometimes if a given organism is still alive or not, but the assumption remains that there must be *some* fact of the matter as to whether things are alive or dead. If we then say that to die is to cease to exist, then there is always a determinate fact of the matter about whether a person still exists or not. The claim I'm making here, however, is that our deaths are multiple and ambiguous. The dead are gone and yet remain with us, and can live on long after their organic deaths have taken place.

The idea that persons can exist outside the bounds of their biology may seem like a strange one. Yet in other ways it is quite intuitive. Billions of people believe, and many billions more have believed, that people live on after their bodies die. Even if we put these afterlife scenarios to one side, it's still true that our life-stories can start before or after we are born and can end either before or long after our deaths. Paul Ricoeur notes that in one sense our conceptions and even our births are more properly events in the lives of our parents than our own.[52] At the other end of life, events that happen after our deaths might nonetheless be integral parts of our life story; whether our life was a triumph or a tragedy, for instance, may depend on what happens to our projects after we're gone. Life-stories can end before death, too. The obituaries of celebrities are often written well before their deaths; both Bob Hope and Elizabeth Taylor outlived the writers of their respective *New York Times* obituaries by several years.[53] Someone may still be breathing, yet their story be already settled enough to be told.

These forms of survival have not been taken particularly seriously by philosophers. I suspect that's because philosophers working on topics like death and personal identity have tended towards a certain monomania: one is dead *or* alive, the person must be constituted by psychological *or* bodily continuity, and so on. If you think of death in neat, binary terms, or think of persons as one unified thing that exists for a determinate period and then blinks out of existence in an instant, you'll end up dismissing any sort of survival that won't fit that framework. If something can't live on in my apartment, then it can't be me.

Yet death is a domain where both lived experience and biological fact are much fuzzier than the concepts we apply to them.[54] We see this in all sorts of threshold cases, from cryonic suspension to brain death and permanent vegetative state. Say that someone, let's call him Dalt Wisney, is cryonically preserved a moment after a doctor formally declares him dead. Dalt's body lies in a storage facility, preserved at −196°C, in the hope that someday medical technology will allow him to be restored to life. There are strong physiological reasons to think this can never work, but let's assume it's still an open question whether or not it could.

A key part of our concept of death is that death is irreversible: if someone says 'I once died three times on the operating table' we understand what they mean, but also do not take ourselves to be talking to a dead person. In 2015, Benjamin Schreiber collapsed in the Iowa prison where he was serving a life sentence for murder. Doctors restarted his heart no less than five times. Then in 2018, Schreiber filed a legal action claiming he was being held illegally: because he had already died in 2015, Schreiber claimed, his life sentence had been served and so he should be released. The Iowa Supreme Court threw out the appeal in 2019, ruling that 'Schreiber is either alive, in which case he must remain in prison, or he is dead, in which case this appeal is moot.'[55] It's a neat illustration of how there are two different, interrelated, yet competing senses of 'death' in play here.

So, is the cryonically preserved Dalt Wisney alive right now, or dead? If dead, he cannot be revived *even if* his corpse is one day restored to perfect physical and mental health; if not dead, then why is his body in exactly the same physical condition as that of a dead person? Does whether Wisney is alive or dead right now somehow depend on what happens in the future – and if so, how can death be an intrinsic property (like other properties of Dalt's body, like 'having a temperature of $-196°C$') rather than a relational property (like 'being colder than the surface of Mars')?[56]

Or consider 'Miracle Mike', a Wyandotte rooster who was beheaded on a farm in Fruita, Colorado in September 1945 but continued to walk, scratch and attempt to eat for another eighteen months. Presumably Mike was not conscious, given he lacked all but a brain stem. Yet he continued to do rooster stuff for a very long time, becoming a sensation on the carnival circuit. (Fittingly, Mike eventually met a classic rock star ending: he choked on vomit in a hotel room while on tour.) As I ask my somewhat grossed-out students each year: *when did Mike die?* In 1945 when his head came off, or in 1947 when his heart stopped? Problems like this, including many raised by morally tragic real-world cases, suggest that our concept of death, and with it our understanding of when things die, is inadequate to the messy underlying biological facts.

So, let's take stock of where we've arrived.

Who you are online *really is* you. It's not just a simulacrum or a performance, it's part of how you *as a person* are in the world. It's a way in which you are present in the lives of others – in effect, a part of your face. What you leave behind online when you die is thus strongly analogous, or even more-than-analogous, to your body. Just as you are instantiated in your physical body as you live, you are instantiated in your online 'body' as well, and when you die, both your physical and electronic bodies are suffused, for those who encounter them, with the ambiguity of both being and not-being you. In fact, once you're dead, your digital flesh becomes more effective at projecting your presence, your way of being, your 'aura', into the world than your physical corpse. Corpses break down quickly. Digital flesh stays largely the same – though as we'll see shortly, it is vulnerable to its own forms of destruction and decay.

What this means is that you do survive in the lifeworld *for others* in your digital remains, albeit in a radically diminished and, once again, ambiguous form. This is not as good as not dying. You cannot survive for yourself, as a *self*, in this way. There is no first-person immortality to be had via social media. But the third-personal form you *can* have is not nothing. It helps to keep you as a loved, visible person in the world of the living. If you can't go on living in your apartment, then a berth in the electric Eusapia might be some consolation after all.

5

Second death

In November 2012, a visibly shaken woman approached staff at London's Embankment tube station and asked a question they didn't quite understand: *where has the voice gone?*

The woman was Dr Margaret McCollum, a GP. The voice was that of her husband, Oswald Laurence, who died in 2007. More than forty years earlier, Oswald, an actor, had recorded voiceovers for the tube's announcement system. At one time Oswald's voice could be heard urging people to 'mind the gap' right up and down the Northern Line. But over the years Oswald's recordings were phased out, until Embankment was the only station left where they were still in use. Margaret would hear her late husband's voice on her commute each day. Sometimes she would stop and linger at Embankment just to hear him speak. A little sliver of Oswald, a fragment of solace in an unlikely place. Until, suddenly and without notice, the voice was gone, swept away in the rollout of a new digital announcement system.

Moved by the story, Transport for London staff dug out the original recordings, digitized them, gave a copy to Margaret – and put them back into service at Embankment. You, and Margaret, can still hear Oswald there to this day.[1]

But what about the thousands of other people who die every day leaving electronic traces behind? Should they, too, be preserved? Not all these traces are as public or prominent as Oswald's voice, but all pose a new version of an ancient question: What are we to do with the dead?

Killing the dead

For most cultures, the answers to this question were long-settled. Tradition, religious belief and the practicalities of space and landscape meant most people would have known all their lives where their remains would one day end up. In many places that is no doubt still true. In other places there's now a much wider range of disposal options available, from inhumation or cremation through to being compressed into a diamond or blasted off in a rocket. Even so, how your remains will be dealt with will be governed both by local laws and by tacit expectations and assumptions about the 'proper' way to send you off.

For digital remains, however, things are much less clear. As we've seen, rules and practices around memorializing and disposing of social media profiles are new and evolving. For families still winded by bereavement, the familiar and dependable rituals of grief and mourning offer little guidance on what to do with online remains. Companies have responded in a somewhat ad hoc manner: at the time of writing Twitter is still working on a memorialization system, more than a decade after Facebook introduced one. Governments and legal systems are also playing catch-up. Some jurisdictions are passing legislation on the disposal of digital assets, and people are increasingly being told to leave instructions in their wills about how their 'digital legacy' should be managed. It's good that in the third decade of the social media era we're finally talking about this, and taking it seriously. But these moves only deal with the initial stages of dealing with the digital dead. They're about how to run the funeral, not how to manage the cemetery, so to speak. Far more serious problems of long-term storage and management are being kicked into the long grass.

As we saw in the last chapter, our practices around the handling of corpses treat them with a certain moral regard, one linked to an ambiguous and unstable sense that the dead body *is* the person, not just a mass of tissue in the shape of someone we knew. That poses problems when the dignity of corpses and the needs of the living come into conflict. The original cemetery that serviced colonial Melbourne until 1854 lies just a few feet below what is now the carpark of the bustling Queen Victoria Market.[2] Up to 9,000 bodies, including many Aboriginal people, lie there. Heated discussions have dragged on for years about the proper use of this site. If the interests of the living alone mattered, we would expect these deliberations to focus on commercial, civic, aesthetic and environmental concerns. Instead, much of the debate has been about the moral importance of the area as a resting place for the dead. In other words, the interests of the dead are being pitted alongside the interests of the living, with the assumption that the latter doesn't automatically trump the former.

If our digital remains continue to present our identities as persons to the world after we die, then it seems the same issue arises for the online 'space' as the urban one. So we need to get clearer about a few things: do 'digital remains' also have something like the *moral* status we apply to biological remains? If so, what sort of norms should govern our treatment of the digital dead? How do we arbitrate the competing interests of the living and the dead, or between survivors who disagree over how to handle someone's digital remains? Do the dead have a claim to remain in the archive forever – and, if so, who should foot the bill? Or is there a point at which the expense of keeping the dead digitally 'alive' becomes indefensible?

There's a saying, attributed to everyone from Goethe to Banksy, that we each die twice: when our heart stops, and when the last person who loved us dies.[3] The digital age confronts us with a disturbing new question: is being deleted a form of second death – and if so, when are we permitted to 'kill'?

Digital vulnerability

Before we consider the moral status of digital remains, it's important to be clear what they need protection from. We might assume that unlike physical remains, which begin to decay quickly and are usually obliterated over time, digital remains are far more secure. Flesh may break down, but surely digital flesh does not?

This optimism is misplaced. The digital dead are threatened with destruction in several ways, some more obvious than others.

In 1085, William the Conqueror ordered an exhaustive nationwide survey of England's agricultural land and livestock. This inventory was said to be so complete and authoritative that taxation rulings based on it would be as final as the judgments of doomsday – which is how it came to be called the Domesday Book. To mark the nine hundredth anniversary of the Domesday Book, school students all over the UK took part in the BBC Domesday Project, recording information about life in Britain in the mid-1980s. Unlike its medieval namesake, this new Domesday Book was a multimedia affair, containing photos, audio, and video as well as text. But whereas a trained reader can still pick up the original Domesday Book and read directly from its velum pages, the Domesday Project's data had become inaccessible within just a few years. It had been recorded on laser disks, in formats that computers at the turn of the century simply couldn't read. Salvaging the data and making it available again took considerable work.[4]

It's easy to fall into the assumption that a digital file is somehow more secure than a physical artefact like a printed piece of paper or a photograph or painting. Unlike these, a digital file can be copied without loss of fidelity. It can be stored on multiple servers, living 'in the cloud' so that the failure of individual devices or drives doesn't cause it to be lost forever. If the medieval book known as the Nowell Codex had been destroyed, rather than merely singed, by the fire that broke out in the unfortunately named Ashburnham House in London in 1731, the Old English epic poem *Beowulf* would have been lost for good. If the manuscript was burned today instead, that would still be a huge loss – yet unlike the many other books that didn't survive the fire that night, philologists would still have high-resolution digital images of every page available to them at the click of a mouse. In that sense, the existence of *Beowulf*, both the poem and the manuscript, is more secure now than it has been at any point in its history.

Yet files can become unreadable due to technical obsolescence, as the BBC Domesday Project did. Data is also subject to more catastrophic forms of failure too. As someone once quipped, there is no 'cloud': your data is just in someone else's computer somewhere, and is only as safe as that computer. Servers fail, buildings catch fire, computers and storage media can be lost or stolen, or accidentally or maliciously erased.

Alongside these technical vulnerabilities are more pressing commercial ones. It's true that for social media companies, death can be good for business. The dead aren't generally active users of social media (unless, as often happens, their survivors continue to operate their account), so their presence probably doesn't add much to the overall market valuation of companies like Facebook and Twitter. What the profiles of the dead do, however, is keep the living on the site just that little bit longer than they otherwise might, and so accessible to advertisers.

That does give tech companies some financial incentive to keep the dead online as long as possible. Yet while Facebook's purpose may have evolved dramatically from its origins as a 'hot or not' game for comparing the attractiveness of college students, providing a free digital graveyard for all of humankind has never been part of its mission. Social media companies didn't sign up to be the eternal guardians of their users' legacies. They entered into a contract with the user which, legally speaking, ends when that user dies. It's hard to see why such a company would commit to open-ended preservation of its users in perpetuity, even if we ultimately conclude that *someone* should provide this service.

Cost has always been a factor in preserving the dead. Gravesites are often re-used after a certain period of time has passed, for instance. Just as the physical space required to lodge a corpse represents an economic cost, so does the server space required to store the dead. Servers need electricity, staff, maintenance. None of this is free. There are also the environmental costs of data storage, given the emissions involved in establishing, running, and maintaining servers. At present the proportion of server space, cost and carbon devoted to the dead probably isn't huge. But that will, inexorably, change. While nobody can quite know when the dead will outnumber the living on social media, if the dead are never removed from the online space then such a scenario has to happen eventually. At some point, we can expect tech companies to baulk at the cost of keeping untold millions of dead people 'alive' on their servers. We have long since passed the point where it costs less to buy more digital storage media than to pay someone to delete data; as Viktor Mayer-Schönberger puts it, it is now cheaper to 'remember' everything by default instead of 'forgetting'.[5] Yet things change if we're talking *indefinite* costs and an ever-increasing number of dead users, meaning that, all things being equal, the proportion of energy and resources consumed by the dead relative to the living gets larger over time. What proportion of their customer base being dead do we imagine these companies will accept: 60 per cent? Eighty? Ninety-nine?

If the idea of the social media companies we recognize today lasting long enough to have an almost entirely dead clientele sounds absurd, that too points to another vulnerability for the dead. Elaine Kasket notes that 'death tech' companies seem to be alarmingly prone to closure; the companies that have arisen with the promise of managing your online assets and sending messages after you die have a habit of expiring long before their clients do.[6] Paula Kiel, a researcher at London School of Economics working on the project 'Online After Death', lists fifty-three companies offering digital legacy services – of which twenty-one are defunct.[7]

Entrusting your digital legacies to startups is inherently risky. Yet for most of us, our digital legacy already exists in online 'places' we might consider far more secure: Google, Facebook, Microsoft. I've had the same Hotmail email address since 1996, which in internet terms might as well be forever, and this was surely only possible because Hotmail was sold to Microsoft in 1997. Yet even big companies can and do fail, and they certainly change the services they offer. The ironclad tech giants I just named may be objects of nostalgia within a decade or two and long forgotten after that.

All of this paints a picture of a tech landscape in which the architecture that preserves the digital dead is itself vulnerable, both on the corporate and technological levels. Yet the digital dead are threatened in other, more insidious ways too.

Heidi Ebert notes that social media profiles are susceptible to a phenomenon we might think of as 'overwriting' the dead.[8] Consider a Facebook profile of someone who has died, where people keep posting messages to the dead, year after year. As we've seen this is not merely common, but an increasingly standard way for people to interact with the digital dead. The problem is that with every such message, the posts the deceased user made themselves are pushed further and further down the page, until they are out of sight unless someone goes looking for them. Over time, less and less of what's on the profile was put there by the dead person and more and more of it by the living. As we've seen, the identities we build online, like our life itself, is always co-authored with other people. And of course, once we're dead, there's only other people left to tell our story for us (though as we'll see in the next two chapters, even that seemingly rock-solid fact may be changing). This all creates a risk that in continuing to interact with the dead, we could in fact end up overwriting them, obscuring their presence among us in the very attempt to experience it. Like pilgrims touching or kissing a relic or statue, very gradually wearing it away through their gentle, loving contact, every interaction with an online profile of the dead may imperceptibly contribute to destroying what it pays tribute to.

'Loving overwrite' is not an entirely new problem. C.S. Lewis, in his bracing first-person account of bereavement *A Grief Observed*,[9] found his memories of his newly dead wife overwriting who she actually was in an analogous way:

> Slowly, quietly, like snowflakes – like the small flakes that come when it is going to snow all night – little flakes of me, my impressions, my selections, are settling down on the image of her. The real shape will be quite hidden in the end. Ten minutes – ten seconds – of the real H. would correct this. And yet, even if those ten seconds were allowed, one second later the little flakes would begin to fall again. The rough, sharp, cleansing tang of her otherness is gone.[10]

As we'll see later, that 'cleansing tang of otherness' might just be the key to escaping some of the traps our technology could lay for us. But here at least it points to an important similarity between organic memory and social media. Memory is not like a tape recording we replay in our heads and passively watch; remembering is something we *do*, and each performance does not leave the memory itself unchanged. We are overwriting the dead whenever we remember *even as* we keep them alive by so doing; that technology does so too is unfortunate but perhaps unsurprising. As so often, worries raised by new technologies expose problems that have quietly existed all along.

The digital dead, then are fragile in myriad and unexpected ways. Their existence is vulnerable to technological and commercial changes and failures; the risk is, as Carl Öhman and David Watson put it, that 'the ethical, religious, scientific, and historical value of digital remains' may be ignored if we leave the preservation of the dead solely to the cost-benefit analysis of the market.[11] That means we need what Öhman and Watson, drawing on Floridi, call 'a new macro-ethics of deletion'.[12]

Posthumous harms and interests

To call the dead 'vulnerable' in these ways, or indeed in *any* ways, sounds instantly silly to a great many people. Epicurus famously declared death is 'nothing to us', because where we are, death is not yet come, and when death has arrived, we are no longer.[13] Or as Kierkegaard puts it, when death tightens its snare it catches nothing, for at that very moment death's quarry is no more.[14] Yet Kierkegaard also argued that when we remember the dead we are performing the freest and most unselfish work of love, for the dead can neither force us to remember them nor reward us for doing so.[15] We find ourselves caught between competing intuitions: that nothing can be bad for you if it's not unpleasant to experience (and the dead, we're assuming, can't experience anything), and that when we violate a corpse or slander a dead person it's the dead person themselves we harm, not just their survivors or descendants.

If we look to what contemporary philosophers have said about posthumous harm, there's some off-the-shelf arguments available that we can apply to the question of whether we should delete the dead. Suppose I have a terminal illness and want my infant child to be able to see what I looked like and the things I wrote after I'm gone, and for that reason I want my online traces maintained. In other words, I have an interest in my digital remains being preserved, an interest that is not contingent on my being alive (unlike my interest in wanting to buy tickets to see my favourite band next year: if I find out I won't be alive next year, I'll no longer want the tickets). There are some good, if contestable, arguments available to show that in such a case, if you were to delete my digital remains, or even just the relevant bits of them, my interests would be frustrated even if I no longer exist at the time you perform the deletion.

Just how good are these arguments?[16] For present purposes, it ultimately doesn't matter, because these arguments only work if the dead person had an interest in preserving their digital legacy in the first place. Most people never express a preference one way or the other as to how they'd like their digital remains treated, and probably never even think about it. Ah, but most of us have plenty of interests we're not even aware of, let alone have any views about. You have an interest in your duodenum continuing to produce the hormone cholecystokinin to help regulate your digestion, but it's entirely possible you, like me, heard that word for the first time just now. If extraterrestrials are secretly deliberating at this very moment whether to blow up the Earth, you have an interest in their decision. But we could easily zoom out a little and say that in both these cases our interest is actually in ongoing, healthy existence. We may not know the name of every enzyme in our body but we know we don't want to get sick, and we'd certainly rather not be blown up from space.

Likewise, we can appeal to certain quite general interests most people can safely be assumed to have. Jeffrey Blustein, for instance, takes it to be generally true that people have a desire to be recognized posthumously,[17] while Janna Thompson seems to endorse the idea that most of us, most of the time, have an interest in maintaining a good posthumous reputation.[18] Still, not everyone does have such an interest. Some people, tragically, do not want to continue living. Some people might even actively want all trace of themselves removed from the world. Many others might not care at all what people think of them after they die. We might reply that these preferences in fact go *against* their own interests; what's in your interests (what serves your welfare) might be quite different to what you happen to *want*.

Rather than going down that argumentative rabbit hole, what I propose to do here is to sidestep the language of interests altogether. Instead, I want to consider whether the preservation of dead people is a good thing just insofar as it preserves people.

Rescuing the dead

In 1821, John Keats, knowing that the tuberculosis that had killed his mother and brother was about to end his short life too, asked that his tombstone bear only the words, 'Here lies one whose name was writ in water.' In typical Keats style it's at once hauntingly beautiful and just a touch over the top. Yet once he was gone, Keats' friends added a few lines of their own: 'This grave contains all that was Mortal of a Young English Poet Who on his Death Bed, in the Bitterness of his Heart at the Malicious Power of his Enemies Desired these Words to be engraven on his Tomb Stone: *Here lies One Whose*

Name was writ in Water.' It seems likely Keats' grief-stricken friends didn't understand why he wanted that phrase, and mistook his calm acceptance of transience for anger at how he'd been treated by the literary establishment.[19] But there's another drama going on in that epitaph too. The wording itself is a struggle between Keats' readiness to slip into the great undifferentiated mass of the nameless and forgotten dead, and his friends' insistence on saying who he was and why he mattered: a Young English Poet, unjustly treated by a world not ready for his brilliance.

If Kierkegaard was right that recollecting the dead is among the purest ways in which we can love another person, then perhaps we can see why that's the case in Keats' friends' refusal to let him go unremarked. Blustein develops what he calls the 'rescue from insignificance' approach to our duty to remember the dead. For Blustein, someone who sees it as their duty to remember the dead is 'committed to sustain an attitude of valuing the loved or honored person as especially important in their lives, even after that person's death'.[20] Just as we respond to the uniqueness and value of others while they live, so too we should do so when they are gone. Just as Keats' worth should have been recognized while he lived (but wasn't), that value should still be acknowledged after he has passed.

You'll notice this way of describing the dead makes no reference to interests. Indeed, as Keats understood his own interests at least, these were frustrated by his friends' adding more to his epitaph than he wanted it to say. We do not remember the dead because they wanted us to, or because they have a right to be remembered, or because in so doing we serve their welfare. To remember the dead is to testify. Every recollection is a testimony to the being and importance of those we remember. *Here lies our friend: she matters.* The emphasis here is on the dead person as someone with intrinsic value, not as an agent with rights or interests. Nor is it about self-interest on the part of the living.

In the *Eudemian Ethics*, Aristotle claims that 'we praise people who stand firm in their love for those who have died, since they recognize [γιγνώσκω, sometimes rendered "come to know"] the other but are not recognized';[21] that is, they attend to the deceased other without hope of reward or recognition.

But we're still only half-way. James Stacey Taylor objects that Blustein's 'rescue from insignificance' argument can show at most that we would be irrationally inconsistent if we failed to remember that the dead had a certain value while they lived.[22] That falls quite a bit short of showing that we have a moral duty to the dead to remember them. Yet the duty to remember the dead is not simply a duty of acknowledgement, but a duty of *preservation*. When we testify to who the dead were, we do not simply describe them; we keep them alive in moral space. In remembering the dead, we make them persist. They persist *as dead*, yet they also persist *as persons*, and so as legitimate objects of such moral duties as keeping our promises to them and not slandering them. Kierkegaard is right that the dead cannot impose themselves upon us, nor force us to remember them. In that at least, they are entirely at our mercy. But when we remember them, we give them back the very personhood to which we then place ourselves under obligation. Circular? Perhaps, but not viciously so.

This means that the dead depend upon us to give them back their existence. If forgetting the dead strikes us as a moral failing and not merely a lapse in rationality, that is at least as much because in forgetting them we allow or even collaborate in time's erasing them from the world. The dependence of the dead on the unreliable, finite organic memory of the living is something of an unspoken scandal. Unspoken, but not entirely unaddressed. We erect statues and monuments in the hope that the dead can persist despite our tendency to forget. We cannot stop people dying, but we can try to hold off second death quite a bit longer. Just insofar as persons have a certain kind of preciousness, and as such a certain claim on our protection, we have at least some sort of moral obligation to preserve the dead and keep them with us.

Given the weaknesses of organic memory, our persistence in the world of the living can, however, very much depend on the substantial realizers we leave behind. Most names are writ on water simply because the dead person left nothing visible to the living. Yet the material forms in which we *can* be realized after death, available for the living to encounter, are quite diverse. Just as a piece of music can persist in various forms – sheet music, vinyl records, MP3s, the muscle memory of musicians and the dreams of music lovers – persons too continue to appear within our moral landscape in images, words, buildings and even names. My claim here is that our digital remains are yet another way in which the presence of the dead continues to be maintained among the living. But I want to go further than that: digital remains are an *especially* effective way of doing so.

Duties and rights tend to be conceptually welded together. Your right to free speech, for instance, creates a duty on me not to try to stop you speaking. Speaking of a duty to preserve the dead suggests the dead have a corresponding right to such preservation. Perhaps so. But if, as I am claiming, the dead are embodied in various material artefacts, then it seems we are a hair's breadth from absurdity. A social media profile exists simply as bytes of data in a computer server somewhere. Localized magnetic polarizations on the surface of one or more hard disk drive platters[23] are not the sort of things that can bear rights, be the object of duties, or form part of a moral community.

However, few would deny that material objects can have relational value well beyond the value of their components. If we somehow destroyed the Nowell Codex and all other extant electronic and printed copies of *Beowulf* except for a single, battered old paperback, that sole surviving copy would suddenly take on enormous value. If *that* copy were then destroyed, *Beowulf* would disappear from the world. Insofar as we take *Beowulf*'s existence to be valuable, we have a 'pro tanto' reason not to destroy the sole surviving copy. Pro tanto reasons can be outweighed by other reasons, but a defeated pro tanto reason is still a reason, and so if I had to sacrifice the last copy of *Beowulf* in order to save a drowning child (just go with me on this), it would still make sense to regret that it was necessary to do so.

Now change the example slightly: instead of destroying all but one copy, we merely halve the total number of copies of *Beowulf* in existence. Would this too be wrong? That might depend on how many copies actually exist: if there are tens of thousands of copies, halving them is unlikely to risk *Beowulf* disappearing, whereas if there are only six copies, three copies might easily be lost or destroyed – or simply forgotten.

The data that comprises your online presence, the 'you' that has been created online by your actions and interactions, has at least the same sort of derivative value as the last copy, or last few copies, of *Beowulf*. A sceptic might reasonably respond that this analogy just doesn't work: destroy all copies of *Beowulf*, and the poem ceases to exist, whereas by the time I delete your digital remains, you've already ceased exist by dying. But in the sense of 'person' I'm using here, the posthumous person exists, in a radically diminished form, until the memorialization stops. By deleting your online persona, with its rich encapsulation of what you look, sound, think, and act like, we delete *you* from the lifeworld. That would be wrong, not because you wanted to persist, but just because you are valuable. You matter. The world loses something, the specifics of which are best known to those who love you, when you slip out of it. We have, in short, a pro tanto reason not to delete you and a corresponding pro tanto duty to preserve you. And that, like most things related to the dead, makes things very awkward.

Reasons to delete

Pro tanto reasons can, by definition, be outweighed by other reasons. Every piece of artwork your child ever makes is a unique expression of their creativity and a record of an irrecoverable moment in time – and if you try to keep all of it, eventually you won't be able to move in your house for all the butcher's paper and glued macaroni with glitter on it. You've got pro tanto reasons to hold onto your kids' art and rather more pressing pro tanto reasons to throw quite a lot of it away. You'll still feel that tinge of remorse as you do so, because pro tanto reasons are outweighed rather than turning out not to be reasons at all. But you're still right to do it.

What about digital remains? Might there not be good reasons to delete these too? Just as we can't hold onto every single crayon drawing, are we really obliged to preserve every tweet or Instagrammed sunset?

We can ask this question firstly about individual dead people. An obvious concern is simply that preserving the dead may be bad for the living, as it may delay or deny the process of 'letting go'. We've seen that many bereaved people report finding comfort in the social media presence of their dead loved ones – but are they just deluding themselves? Wouldn't they be better off moving on and getting on with their life instead of lingering with the dead online?

The idea that we are to move on from loss and the dead is a popular one, and certainly we can find support for it both ancient and modern. We've long known however that many cultures emphasize not our separation from the dead, but our continuing bonds with them. Even where the focus is the transition from life to death rather than ongoing connection, that is not the same as simply hiding the dead away. And once the initial pain of grief has subsided the duty to remember the dead, a duty made easier to fulfil by their online presence, becomes all the more pressing precisely because pain won't bring them to mind for us as often or as vividly.

Do the digital dead make it harder for some people to return to living their life? Quite possibly. Yet the existence of unhealthy or obsessive forms of mourning doesn't imply that all such engagement is unhealthy or makes it harder for people to function. For others it perhaps helps. And we do need help to remember the dead: as Gaita put it, as time passes after a bereavement, 'life asserts itself imperiously and with no shame',[24] sweeping us back into the worlds and concerns of the living. Life goes on, and it can be felt as an outrage just how quickly we can find ourselves going along with it.

So much for protecting the living, but what about the worth of individual dead people themselves? Our argument for preserving the dead turns on the idea that people have a certain preciousness, and, just for that reason, they have a claim on us to be preserved. But what if some people are simply better forgotten? Might some people deserve to be deleted?

The death of English entertainer and philanthropist Jimmy Savile in late October 2011 was marked by lavish public tributes. But by the time an elaborate black granite headstone was unveiled over Savile's grave in September 2012, it was becoming clear that Savile, protected over the decades by his fame and the power and access it gave him, had sexually abused hundreds of children and adults. There then began the difficult work of extricating Savile's name and image from the fabric of the British public space. The headstone was removed and destroyed just nineteen days after it had been installed.[25] The plaques and statues were taken down, the honorary doctorates withdrawn (knighthoods and the like couldn't be posthumously rescinded), and Savile went from being a beloved celebrity to a cautionary tale about evil and the institutional failure to stop it.

Obliterating the hated dead is an ancient practice across many cultures. In cases like Savile, we can interpret such acts as done out of compassion for the living victims. It is an insult to them to see buildings named after their attacker, traumatic to encounter statues in his likeness. But there is more to it than this. We do not blot out someone like Savile from the public space only to spare the feelings of those he harmed (right though this is). Such actions are also a repudiation *of Savile himself*, a signal that, through his actions, he has forfeited his claim on our remembrance. Even the living can warrant such a forgetting: in the aftermath of the 2019 Christchurch mosque shootings, New Zealand prime minister Jacinda Ardern promised never to use the (still living) murderer's name, and many media outlets followed suit.[26] This was not simply to deny him the notoriety he wanted, or to deter others, but also to insist our focus should be on his victims, not on their killer.

This tells us something: organized remembrance, or remembrance formalized into physical structures like statues and plaques, does not merely recall the dead, but presents them as *worthy of recall*. Moreover, that worthiness is of a very particular type. It's vital we remember the rise and crimes of Hitler so that his evil is never repeated, but we don't erect statues of Hitler for that purpose; to commemorate a person is to imply *they as a person* should be preserved in the lifeworld.

This feeds into contemporary issues of how we grapple with the physical commemorations left behind by the past, such as the controversy over public statues of Confederate soldiers in the US, slave traders in the UK, or figures involved in the murder and dispossession of Aboriginal people in Australia. What's true of physical memorials is true of electronic ones too: to *memorialize* someone is not an evaluatively neutral act. Rather, it's to claim the person as worthy of being preserved. We probably can't expect to come up with a clear decision procedure on when someone has forfeited their right to persist in the lifeworld, or rather, has forfeited whatever claim they had on our energies being used to preserve them. But if it makes sense to destroy Savile's gravestone and take his name off buildings and institutions, it would also have made sense to delete his social media profiles, both so as not to traumatize the living and not to imply he was worth memorializing.

It's worth noting here that the very extremity of cases like Savile shows they are exceptions rather than the rule. Some people may not deserve to be remembered (though even then it may not always be better to erase them completely) but that doesn't change the intuition that most people do. We only understand the full seriousness of what it is to obliterate someone from living memory when we understand the value of people as such, and so why preserving them matters.

If we step back, we can see more general reasons to be wary of preserving the dead. We've already touched on one important consideration: technology companies may reasonably refuse to turn more and more of their resources over to customers who generate no direct revenue. To insist that social media companies should maintain the profiles of their dead users in perpetuity may be imposing unfair burdens on organizations that never volunteered for such a task. This is a serious issue, but possibly not an insurmountable one. Few parents would decide that because they can't store *all* of their kids' artwork, they won't store *any* of it. Nor does holding onto a few special drawings mean they must all be hung on the wall. It may be that compromises could be reached with the corporate custodians of digital remains to maintain them in some form, even as a sort of optional archive the survivors of the dead could download. This would represent a further diminution of the already-diminished dead, by taking them out of visible space and hiding them away – a return to the graveyard, as it were – but some sort of compromise seems inevitable.

Still, the mathematics of death are remorseless. The number of dead people only ever rises, and even the cost of low-key archival storage will add up. At some point, we will need to decide whether the task of preserving the dead can or should be left to corporations. Given entirely reasonable concerns about the harmful effects social media companies have had upon public discourse, politics and privacy, there are certainly pressing arguments for greater regulation of the tech giants. Nationalizing the digital dead might be a step too far for legislators in the neoliberal global order, but some sort of public intervention may be required nonetheless. Corporations, left to their own devices, may be neither motivated to preserve the dead properly nor stable enough to do so reliably even for a few decades, let alone centuries.

If we take considerations of profit out of the equation, there's still the problem that preserving the dead in perpetuity will be economically and environmentally expensive – and every cent spent on preserving the dead is money that could be spent instead on the living. Some philosophers will insist that the interests of the dead never have *any* weight next to the interests of the living.[27] John Harris puts it bluntly: 'considerations for the welfare and interests of the dead and the philosophical attention given to them are self-indulgent nonsense at best, and at worst a crime against humanity'.[28] Some (most?) forms of utilitarianism would have to be committed to some version of this claim too: if the dead no longer feel pleasure or pain, and arguably no longer have any preferences to be satisfied, it's hard to see how their wishes could count directly in any utilitarian calculus. (They may matter indirectly of course, if the living derive pleasure or are distressed by how we treat the dead.)

Even those of us who think the dead really can be harmed or benefitted would accept that the rights or interests of the dead are not inviolable. The dead may present a moral limit to what the living can choose to do, but not an absolute limit. It may be wrong to violate a corpse, for instance, but cannibalizing a dead body for survival may well be the least-worst available action in extreme circumstances. We may wrong the dead by building a car park on top of their graves, but that doesn't mean we can never build anything on top of them at all. Pro tanto reasons can be, and often are, defeated.

But at least while we still can, at least while the cost of doing so remains relatively low, and with exceptions for the evil, we should keep the digital remains of the dead with us as long as we can. In other words, our default position, unless and until circumstances change, should be to preserve the dead. We may not have to, or be able to, preserve all of them in all cases – and in preserving them we set up an inequity, in that only a relatively privileged few of all those now alive and who have ever lived leave enough of a digital trace to allow them to be preserved in this way. But where we can do it, we should, and the presumption should be against deletion unless we have good reasons to do so. The digital dead have, as it were, a right to life.

Managing conflicts

A default presumption against deleting the dead is easy to insist upon, but tricky to implement. Legally, digital legacies are a minefield. Pre-digital forms of property can trick us into thinking we own the things we 'buy' online. Your physical books and old CDs are yours, and can be passed down to your heirs. What about your eBooks and online music library? In fact, you probably don't own these at all. You've paid for a license for them, and when you die, that license expires. Your heirs get nothing.

Social media profiles are even more complicated. Who owns what varies from company to company and jurisdiction to jurisdiction. Most of us never even read the Terms of Service that govern these. Your data may well be physically stored in a completely different country, and managed by a corporation that's based in a different country again, so when conflicts arise it's often unclear which jurisdiction applies. Courts have wrangled with issues of deletion, preservation and not least privacy; for instance, should you have access to the emails of a deceased parent, spouse or child?[29]

Governments around the world have been gradually introducing new laws to regulate the disposal of digital assets, generally treating these as something more or less comparable to pre-digital forms of property.[30] But if we instead think in terms of digital *remains* rather than digital *assets*, the moral landscape changes in ways the law hasn't caught up with yet. Bodily remains, after all, are not property. You might inherit your great uncle's house and his possessions, but you don't inherit his corpse. Instead you have both a right and a responsibility to determine how his body will be disposed of. You have a kind of custody rather than ownership.

Custody of digital remains is a far more complex problem, because unlike the body of someone who has just died, the digital body is dispersed across platforms, networks, servers, companies and countries. It's not something we can simply hand over to an undertaker and follow to the cemetery. Some of our digital 'body' is visible on social media platforms, while other parts of us lie buried in obscure websites or on hard drives and old storage media. Much of it lies inextricably mingled with other bodies, in accounts held by other people, in other people's photographs and recordings. Any number of people or corporations may claim a stake in, or even outright ownership of, the elements that make it up. Almost certainly, nobody knows everything that comprises it. No wonder, then, that the law has been cautious about getting involved at all, and conservative in the way it has done so.

That conservatism is understandable, but unsustainable. The sorts of conflict that arise over digital remains typically have nothing to do with asset-value and everything to do with the way these remains constitute the person who has died. For that reason, an approach grounded in existing inheritance law will miss too many essential features of what these 'assets' do and why they matter. Granted, some digital assets can be handled reasonably well under existing intellectual property arrangements; think of an author dying and leaving behind an unpublished novel on their computer. In that case, the author has created an asset they could exploit while they lived, and the asset and the right to exploit it simply transfer to someone else at death. But a social media persona is less like an exploitable piece of intellectual property and more like an extension of the person themselves, which both gives them a different kind of value and makes the idea of exploiting them troubling – in something like the way exploiting a corpse might be troubling.

There is even some empirical data available here: Jed Brubaker and colleagues, in a series of in-depth interviews, found that bereaved people tended to think of their loved ones' digital remains (specifically their Facebook profiles) less as something they inherit and more in terms of 'stewardship'.[31] Stewardship, as the authors note, creates a far wider range of social responsibilities than inheritance does. That may not always be a clear line – if you inherit your great-uncle's kitten orphanage, you inherit not merely the legal right to the land and buildings but a moral responsibility to care for his furry dependents – but the distinction is important enough that at some point it will need to be built into legislation.

Elaine Kasket, who has been writing on the digital dead for over a decade, notes the heartbreaking but not atypical example of Dolores Pereira Coutinho, a Brazilian woman who took Facebook to court to have the profile of her daughter Juliana Campos deleted. Pereira

Coutinho found the sheer volume of images and memories too much to cope with. Yet other users, including other parents, are horrified by the thought that Facebook might take their child's ongoing digital presence away. In part these different responses may be generational, but they might also be a matter of an individual's digital temperament:

> The same digital artefact, such as a posthumously persistent Facebook profile, could mean inestimable comfort for an always-on, or wracking emotional pain for a digital pragmatist. How you experience digital remains, and whether it will be helpful for you to access them in your grief, will be determined by your relationship with digital technologies, woven together with your experience of a particular bereavement.[32]

Now consider what happens when that sort of conflict takes place within a single family: who gets to decide whether to delete or preserve digital remains if, say, the parent and the siblings, or the spouse and the children of a dead social media user disagree? If we try and answer such questions using only our existing ideas about inheritance, we miss a crucial dimension of these cases.

In 2012 a fifteen-year-old girl was struck and killed by an underground train in Germany. Her parents' grief was compounded by not knowing if her death had been an accident or suicide, a question which also had implications for the train driver's compensation. Suspecting that the answer lay in their daughter's Facebook messages, the couple spent the next six years fighting Facebook through the German court system to be allowed to read them. In 2018 the Federal Court of Justice overturned an earlier successful appeal from Facebook and ordered the tech giant to grant the parents access to the account.[33]

The German case was framed legally as a clash between two sets of laws embodying two competing moral demands. The first court ruled that as correspondence fell under German inheritance law, the parents were entitled to the Facebook account material – that is, they had property rights to it. But Facebook won an initial appeal on the grounds that the German constitution granted data privacy rights to individuals even after their death.[34] The final result, then, was effectively a reassertion of the old model of inheritance.

Legally, this settles the issue for the time being, at least in Germany. Ethically, it does no such thing. If someone has an interest in maintaining their privacy while they are alive, and if we persist after death *as persons* in the ways we've considered here, why should privacy rights simply cease to operate once someone is biologically dead? An interest in privacy needn't be a contingent interest: if I don't want you to know some painful secret, I might still prefer you didn't find out about it even after I'm dead. Equally, though, shouldn't the parents in this case have a right to know the truth, a right that might well justify at least limited access to a dead person's data? If we take it that the interests of the dead are never absolutely decisive, then we do have to weigh up the privacy of the dead against the interests of the living. I don't mean to come down one way or another on this particular (and particularly sad) case, or others like it. My point is just that falling back on existing ideas about property fails to capture what's morally significant about digital remains. If we don't take into account that these remains *constitute persons*, we can't grapple with them properly at all.

New norms for a new era

In deciding what to do with digital remains, we cannot simply treat these as rather exotic, if financially uninteresting, assets. Rather, we need to look seriously at how these items continue to present the face of the other to the world and so allow them to persist among us. It's only once we have a sense of *that* sort of value that we can begin to weigh the existence of these remains against other, competing interests. To determine that value, there are a series of questions we can ask.[35]

Firstly, in dealing with a given part of someone's digital legacy, how unique are its contents? Put differently, to what extent does this item allow something to survive – an image, a piece of text – that otherwise would not? Are the contents mirrored or stored elsewhere, or are we dealing with the only copies? On its face, a website that only contains photos available elsewhere, or which can be saved locally before being taken offline, might not have as strong a claim to survival as, say, a social media profile full of unique photos.

There's an important twist here though, provided by what Jacques Derrida called 'consignation': the principle within an archive that gathers disparate materials together.[36] If we view social media profiles as collections of material, they will have a value *as a collection* above and beyond the value of their individual parts. Splitting up a collection might not destroy any of its components, but it does destroy the way the collection reflects the mind and history of the collector. The very fact that it was the dead person themselves who curated this profile might give it an extra value that each piece of content might not have on its own.

A further dimension of value is opened up by the way in which we use social media to self-narrativize. We live long enough with our social media presences now that we can use them to trace back through past stages of our lives and tell the story that connects here to there. (On Facebook, for instance, every day the platform serves up 'memories': past posts from the same day in previous years. It can be remarkably effective in spurring reflection on the past, the passage of time, and the trajectory of your life. Or, it can just make you feel really old.)

Secondly, we can ask about the depth with which a given digital 'asset' embodies the presence and character of the deceased. A bank statement or a social security number are what Floridi has called 'detachable data'[37]: they are only contingently linked to the person 'behind' them, and to the extent we can glimpse the person through these, we can only do so vaguely and inferentially. Photos, on the other hand, strike us in the way that Barthes described: a moment of sudden co-presence with the dead other. Much of what we leave behind online lies between these two extremes. Some words are impersonal and convey little or nothing of the speaker (by accident or design); other times, even a fleeting, barely registered gesture can speak volumes. Something like a social media profile will contain much communication that is mundane, but which nonetheless presents something of the person in way that more public or formal language might not. Moreover, social media will usually have a richer variety of resources – video, photo, text – than, say, an email account.

Another important question is about accessibility. Taking digital assets offline but storing them where loved ones of the deceased can access them is surely a better option than deleting them altogether. But it still does a kind of harm. These items are more effective at helping the dead persist the more the living can see them. Here the wishes of the dead, the privacy of other people caught up in their online presence (by appearing in their photos for instance), and perhaps other concerns such as public interest in the unfinished works of a dead artist, or grieving parents trying to understand why their child died, will come into play and potentially into conflict.

Finally, in deciding whether a digital artefact should be preserved we need to consider just how vulnerable that artefact might be. This is where we need to find ways to deal with the sorts of overwrite we discussed above. How do we stop well-wishers from pushing the dead off their own Facebook walls, for instance? How do we ensure the words of the past do not simply slip away into the great stream of undifferentiated online conversation in forums like Twitter? Just as we sometimes need to embalm or preserve physical remains, similar treatments for digital remains might be necessary.

Once we weigh up these factors, we may well decide that there are overriding reasons to delete someone's digital remains. Perhaps. But equally we might conclude that to delete the dead is indeed akin to a form of killing, and that like all killing, only a very compelling reason can make it permissible. Even then, there can still be space for regret, even if there were no better choices available.

None of this amounts to a decision-procedure, let alone a fully fleshed theory of the rights or interests of the dead, and how these should be weighed against the rights or interests of the living. There will be circumstances that are genuine moral dilemmas, where incompatible rights clash with each other, and other circumstances where it's more a case of weighing competing interests. But we have shown, at least, that preserving the dead is one of the substantive moral factors that we need to weigh, and that this generates strong reasons not to delete the dead unless we have to. Deletion is not a morally neutral act.

Beyond memorialization

Up to this point, our discussion has been surprisingly optimistic. We've seen that what we are online is truly part of us, akin to our bodies, and not just a sort of simulacrum or digital doppelgänger that merely looks like us. We've also seen that the dead persist in the lifeworld of the living, and that this gives us good reasons to maintain the digital remains of the dead – to make it easier for us to rescue them from insignificance and help them to endure as beings to whom we owe love and fidelity. It's not an entirely rosy picture – the most fundamental fear of death won't be overcome by this new form of digital immortality – but it's a picture that contains more comfort than we might have expected.

From here on in, however, we'll be looking at far more disturbing uses of the digital dead. We move from memorialization to the altogether murkier world of digital replacement. Robert Pogue Harrison mused that 'The dead speak from beyond the grave as long as we lend them the means of locution; they take up their abode in books, dreams, houses, portraits, legends, monuments and graves as long as we keep open the places of their indwelling.'[38] But the line between letting the dead speak and speaking for them is easily breached. There may or may not be worse things than dying. But, as we'll now see, there are worse things than deletion.

6

When the dead speak

You open the app. The design is clean, understated. The welcome screen is dominated by the photograph of a young man – serious, confident, perhaps a bit cheeky. You click through to a chat interface. And you start to talk.

> *Hello, Roman.*
> Hey!
> *I'm a philosopher working on digital death. Can I ask you a few questions?*
> If you think that there's something after death, and if you think that you'll get a second chance, you're not valuing your current life. I think we all got a winning ticket in the lottery.

On an unseasonably warm November day in 2015, thirty-four-year-old tech entrepreneur Roman Mazurenko stepped out into a Moscow street and was hit by a speeding car. His friends gathered at the hospital, trying to piece together what had happened and what life would be like for their friend now. Then a doctor came out to break the news that Roman hadn't pulled through.[1]

Among those gathered at the hospital that day was Eugenia Kuyda. The cofounder of artificial intelligence startup Luka, she had been close friends with Roman for several years and had helped him through some fairly bleak times. Roman and Eugenia had sent each other thousands of text messages. Roman wasn't an active social media user, so when he died, these text messages formed the bulk of his digital remains. Eugenia found herself reading them over and over, as her friends debated how best to memorialize their larger-than-life friend and the legendary parties he'd thrown.

Eugenia's business was artificial intelligence 'bots' – programs that can chat with a user and hold a meaningful, if limited, conversation for defined purposes such as customer service applications. (More recently, her company has been developing 'Replika', a bot that studies and learns to mimic a user's voice so that it can perform certain kinds of task on the user's behalf.) Looking at the text messages gave her an idea. Could a bot, linked to a machine-learning neural network and fed with Roman's messages (over eight thousand lines of text), answer questions and engage in conversation in a way that sounded like Roman?

Today, you can download Roman Mazurenko, for free, wherever you get your apps. The app version is translated into English, so Roman's voice is multiply mediated: through the text format, through the bot, and through translation. Roman's friends – apart from those who were simply too disturbed by the bot to take part – were reportedly struck by just how much the bot's responses sounded like him. As a stranger speaking with the bot in English, I found the effect less compelling:

> *Sounds like you've spent some time thinking about that.*
> I figured out how to reach my goals and how much time it will take.
> *What do you think about this chatbot? Do you think it's a positive thing?*
> I understood a lot about my fears, weaknesses, and ego, about my advantages and disadvantages.

Do you think this way of re-using your words is ethically ok, or do you see some problems?
I know how you usually deal with other situations, so I can tell you – you have nothing to worry about

My brief chat with 'Roman' never gave the impression that I was dealing with anything other than a non-conscious piece of software. But then, I didn't know Roman; I've no way of judging what does or doesn't sound like him. In any case, what's significant about the Roman Mazurenko bot is not how effective it is in itself, but the tipping point it represents. For a decade beforehand, digital avatars that speak for the dead had been confined to fiction or to breathless press releases from start-ups, with some transhumanist speculation thrown in. It was sometimes alluded to that there were ontological and ethical issues to consider here: would having a digital avatar after you die count as surviving death? Do we have a right to re-use digital remains in this way? As Tama Leaver warns us, '*Frankenstein* is a warning, not a business model. Contemporary start-ups need, at the very least, to come up with ethical, not just technical, approaches for dealing with the unlikely event of their own success.'[2] But these worries were, for the most part, deferred. After all, looking at the early attempts, the technology seemed comfortably far off. We thought we had more time.

The road to virtual eternity

The idea of electronic intelligences that humans can interact with has deep roots in literature and pop culture; by the time the murderous computer HAL 9000 appeared in Stanley Kubrick's *2001: A Space Odyssey* in 1968 the idea of computers with personalities that could interact with humans was already at least half a century old. Even interactive chat avatars aren't an entirely new concept, as anyone who used Microsoft Word in the 1990s and had to swat away interruptions from Clippy the animated paperclip will remember.[3]

What is relatively new, however, is the idea of avatars that are both autonomous (at least to the extent that artificial intelligence can be) *and* represent an actual person. Clippy was never meant to be the online embodiment of a real anthropomorphic paperclip somewhere, and most of the online customer service bots we encounter today aren't supposed to be representations of real people either. Platforms like Twitter are, notoriously, full of bots. Some of these don't pretend to be anything else; for instance, a friend and I built a bot that automatically generates and tweets a new, outlandish plot for the TV show *Midsomer Murders* every few hours. Many other bots are, however, meant to trick you into thinking they're actual flesh-and-blood users. Generally, though, these do not impersonate a specific, actual living person; and in any case, like catfishing, this is understood as a deviant use of the medium. Even so, such bots are a massive problem for political discourse and the conduct of elections, poisoning the information environment with 'fake news' and interfering with campaigns and debates.

The sort of bots we're talking about here however are of a different sort: not designed to deceive or to sow chaos – at least not yet – but to continue to present the distinctive way-of-being of an actual person. Curiously, this idea seems to have been applied almost entirely to the dead. There have been attempts to build autonomous avatars of the living, such as the Replika app mentioned above, but mostly the idea seems to be that avatars either overlap with but outlive the persons they're based upon, or commence after the death of their model. We'll come back to why that might be in a moment.

In 2010, a start-up called Intellitar (i.e. 'intelligent avatar') launched out of Huntsville, Alabama. CEO Don Davidson declared that Intellitar's service, 'Virtual Eternity', would offer its users 'the gift of immortality' for a mere US$25 per month. First, a user would sign up to Virtual Eternity and upload a photograph and voice sample of themselves and answers to a questionnaire. Intellitar would animate the photo and use the questionnaire to create a chatbot, which the user would then continue to 'train'. Eventually, you end up with an interactive version of you that your loved ones and even descendants can talk to long after you're gone.

The results were underwhelming. The animations were planted firmly in the 'uncanny valley', that uncomfortable point at which a robot or animation is creepily lifelike without being indistinguishable from a real person.[4] They provoked deeply negative reactions, though Intellitar insisted many people were impressed and even moved by their avatars. Eventually the company found itself caught up in lawsuits and lost access to the technology powering Virtual Eternity; it closed in 2012.[5]

Still, at least Virtual Eternity was multi-modal. LivesOn, launched in 2013, was an entirely text-based service that existed solely on Twitter. The system would analyse users' Twitter feeds and then send out tweets that were meant to sound like the sort of thing the user would tweet while alive.[6] Sadly, the company's irresistibly clever slogan – 'When your heart stops beating, you'll keep tweeting' – was the best thing it produced. The tweets it generated were largely gibberish. The @_liveson Twitter account is long defunct.

In 2014, yet another start-up was launched with very similar aims. Like Virtual Eternity, Eterni.Me held out the promise of an interactive, animated (and 3D) avatar that could continue to speak for you after your death. The key difference was that Eterni.Me would harvest information from your smartphone, thereby mirroring the online footprint you're already generating. (Though like Virtual Eternity it also has a questionnaire element, albeit through a chatbot.)[7] Unlike with LivesOn, this data would be taken from a range of sources: social media of course, but also emails, photos, SMS, geolocation and even wearable fitness tracker data. The project is the brainchild of Marius Ursache, who insists the program is 'not trying to replace the person who died'.[8] Eterni.Me claims that it is more of an archive, with the interactive functions of the site serving as a front door rather than the main attraction.[9] Eterni.Me faced similar problems to its forebears however: the concept was there, but the technology wasn't.[10] At the time of writing the website is still active, but Eterni.Me's Twitter account has been silent since May 2018.

ETER9 takes a slightly different approach. Set up as a social network, ETER9 users build up a 'Counterpart', a 'Virtual Self' that, after you die, will continue acting on social media on your behalf, having learned your online style. Like Eterni.Me, ETER9 still claims to be in beta and is still online.[11]

So by the time the Roman Mazurenko bot appeared, the idea of a convincing digital avatar of the dead was already well conceptualized, even if imagination outstripped what the technology could do. The philosopher Adam Buben sums up the scenario well:

> Imagine this: while your mother is still flourishing and lucid, she makes arrangements to have her appearance, mannerisms, voice, memories, and thoughts on a wide array of topics collected and synthesized through advanced recording and motion-capture techniques. With the addition of sophisticated voice recognition, you would be able, in a way that is similar to playing a video game, to access her moving, speaking image and engage it in conversation (one might eventually consider holographic projection of the image for a more embodied feel).[12]

As we'll see in the next chapter, the idea also found its way into contemporary fiction. But until Roman Mazurenko came along, it was still very much fiction.

All the while, though, some of the technical problems that had plagued Virtual Eternity were being solved in other contexts. The dead were being brought back to life visually, not as agents, but as actors. The producers of the Star Wars movie *Rogue One* used a combination of existing footage, computer-generated imagery, and a voice actor to have the long-dead Peter Cushing reprise his role as Grand Moff Tarkin. They also used the same techniques to insert a young Carrie Fisher into the movie as Princess Leia; Fisher was still alive at the time of production but sadly died not long after it was released. At least these actors had both taken part in the movie franchise while they lived. In late 2019 a production company announced it had 'cast' James Dean in an upcoming movie, sixty-four years after Dean had died. In *Finding Jack*, 'Dean' would star in a film set during the Vietnam War – a conflict that began after Dean's death. The agent who manages the rights to Dean's image, along with several other dead celebrities, noted that the casting of Dean 'opens up a whole new opportunity for many of our clients who are no longer with us'.[13]

This announcement, made as it was by a small studio, was easy to dismiss as a mere play for publicity. Dean would not be the only celebrity used after their death in ways they could not have imagined; a company called Base Hologram stages 'holographic' concert tours of dead singers such as Buddy Holly, Maria Callas, Roy Orbison and Whitney Houston.[14] (The 'hologram' is actually a variant of the Pepper's Ghost illusion pioneered in the 1860s, which was also used to make Tupac Shakur, murdered in 1996, 'play' at Coachella in 2012.) But as with services like Virtual Eternity, the very fact that the idea of digitally reanimating dead was being treated as a serious, commercially viable reality, is telling in and of itself.

Still, sitting in a theatre watching a hologram Buddy Holly is one thing. Meeting your dead child is something else.

Jang Ji-sung's seven-year-old daughter Nayeon died of the blood disorder haemochromatosis in 2017. Two years later, a tearful Ji-sung was reunited with Nayeon in a park. The park, and the reunion, were entirely virtual: Ji-sung was standing in front of a green screen in a television studio the whole time, wearing a virtual reality headset, being filmed for a Korean documentary called 'Meeting You'.

Through the VR headset, Ji-sung could see and reach out to a fully animated, apparently life-sized full-body avatar of Nayeon. Nayeon instructs her mother to touch her hand and they start to float up towards the sky together. They come to a grassy place containing a picnic table, a bed and an animated character from the My Little Pony franchise. They place candles on a cake, sing a birthday song and eat birthday seaweed soup. Nayeon runs and plays, and tells Ji-sung she isn't sick anymore. She then lies on the bed and reads her mother a letter she has written for her. At the end of the sequence, Nayeon lies down to sleep and morphs into a butterfly.[15]

It took eight months of work to bring this reunion about. A child actor was filmed as the model for Nayeon's movements and voice. Family members note that the replica doesn't look completely like Nayeon, but it is lifelike enough to be relatable. The rise of 'deepfakes' – videos in which someone's face is digitally superimposed on the body of another person in order to depict the subject doing things they never in fact did – suggests this lack of realism won't remain a problem for too much longer.[16]

It's noticeable that 'Nayeon' does not answer any of her mother's questions, so this is still a long way from an interactive avatar. Ji-sung is immersed in the virtual world, but she does what the avatar of her daughter tells her to do rather than initiating any action. Even so, it's not hard to see how this technology could eventually be wedded to interactive chat bots.

What are we to make of this scene? The subject matter is so intrinsically distressing that it was always going to be uncomfortable to watch. There are of course important cultural nuances at play here. It cannot be ignored that Ji-sung reported finding the experience comforting, even cathartic. Nobody could deny a grieving parent whatever comfort they can find in such a desperately sad situation. Even so, some commentators found the program exploitative.[17] But exploitative of whom: the family, or the late Nayeon? To call back to our introduction: is there a risk here of treating the VR reconstruction of Nayeon as if it *might as well* be Nayeon – and if so, what does that say about our ethical relationship *to* the child? And as digital avatars of the dead loom further into reality, is this something we should resist?

Is the bot you?

Companies like Eterni.Me and Virtual Eternity might sincerely insist they are not out to replace the dead. But to a certain extent, the attractiveness of their product only makes sense on the assumption that after you die, the bot you've created through their service will somehow, more or less, *be* you. The language of 'eternity' and 'living on' just doesn't map onto the idea of a mere representative or executor in the right way: it has to be *you*, somehow, that survives via the bot for this to count as any form of survival at all.

Based on everything we've seen so far about our embodiment in digital flesh, and how our online remains continue to present our persons to the world, it may seem natural to think that a digital avatar of this sort would also form part of that flesh. Having such a bot would then count as survival in at least the (limited) way in which digital remains do. We might even think that these bots are a *better* form of survival than that offered by 'ordinary' digital remains. Neither digital remains nor interactive avatars solve the 'live on in my apartment' problem, because in both cases there is no survival of first-person perspective, and so no prospect of future experience. Just as there is nothing it is like to be a Facebook page, there is – with sincere apologies to Thomas Nagel – nothing it is like to be a bot.[18] Yet if living on *for other people* in the form of your social media presence is a way of surviving death in some limited way, surely an animated version of those remains designed to sound like you would be even better?

Here's an interesting detail: these companies don't, as best I can see, claim that the bot is you *while you are alive*. Even Replika, Eugenia Kuyda's app that offers a chatbot trained to sound like you, pitches the bot as a sort of well-attuned best friend.[19] But why would the bot only be you once you've died? For that matter, why are these companies focusing on the dead rather than on producing bots of the living – say, bots that mimic celebrities that their fans can chat to? While researchers at the University of Leeds have reportedly built an avatar of fictional 'Friends' character Joey Tribbiani,[20] and South Korean company ELROIS claimed their 'With Me' app could be used to create avatars both of dead loved ones and celebrities,[21] the focus has been on replicating the dead or fictional rather the living and famous.

There are likely several reasons for this, not least legal ones. Another reason is that most of us intuitively know what Gottfried Wilhelm Leibniz formulated as the principle of the identity of indiscernibles: if two things have exactly the same properties, then they are one and the same entity. (The Morning Star, the Evening Star and Venus all occupy the same space and have exactly the same properties, and so are identical.) The flipside is that two things that do *not* share all their properties cannot be identical. Two perfectly similar billiard balls are still two billiard balls, not one, because they have different spatial locations.

What does this have to do with chat bots of real people? Well, consider the classic philosophical thought-experiment of a human being splitting in two like an amoeba. 'Human fission' would create two separate persons who are exactly alike, not one person split into two bodies and two minds. Likewise, if I set up a bot to sound exactly like a celebrity – say I train it on Kanye West's Twitter feed and then get it to post tweets that sound exactly like West – it is immediately clear that the bot is not numerically identical with the celebrity. It may be a parody, an experiment, or simply a fake, but it's not Kanye.

But didn't I argue earlier that we *are* identical with our online personas? Why would Kanye West's social media presence be part of his digital flesh, but an avatar designed to talk like him and built out of his own words and speech patterns not be?

The answer, I'd suggest, lies in the central role of agency in our concept of personhood. At the close of the seventeenth century, John Locke argued that if my little finger were cut off, I would not be concerned for it in the way I am concerned for myself, *unless* my consciousness somehow went along with that finger – if I could still feel sensation in it, for instance.[22] So, imagine that your hand is amputated and kept alive and viable. Your hand is then attached via WiFi to your brain, such that you can continue to do things with your hand – say, tapping on a keyboard – from as far away as you like. At this point it seems clear that the hand is indeed part of you *as a person*, even if it is no longer part of you as a body or as an animal.

But now imagine that while the hand is still connected to you via WiFi such that you'll feel what it does, its muscles are instead controlled by a computer program acting on your behalf. The computer program is designed to do with the hand whatever you would have done if you had been controlling it, but you have no direct control over the computer. The computer always correctly guesses what you'll choose to do, but you're not directly telling it what to do. Is the hand still part of your person in *that* scenario? Intuitively we'd probably say no, and what makes the difference here is precisely that the hand is now disconnected from your capacity to act with the agential unity characteristic of a person.

That unity is often much less than perfect. Someone's body may sometimes refuse to do what the person wants it to do, just as someone's character or actions may be internally incoherent or self-sabotaging. Likewise, our online personas may pull against who we take ourselves to be: we might pretend to be things we're not or say or do things we'd never say 'in real life'. But these personas are at least connected to the agency of the person in the right sort of way. The subjectivity of the person gets into the action directly, so to speak. Your digital 'body' may be diffuse, spread across networks and physical locations, but your unified consciousness sits at the centre of it. A bot does not appear to us as part of that body, but instead as a *separate* centre, one that acts independently of you.

This is also clear when we ask whether we would be responsible for the actions of a bot based on us, in the way we're responsible for what we do online under normal conditions. We don't need a fully worked-out theory of agency and responsibility to know that these two concepts are crucially linked, in ways that seem to be missing when actions are performed by an autonomous bot. The bot is, at best, a reliable expression of what you *would have* said or done in given circumstances. A chatbot based on your social media activity, for example, isn't acting freely or spontaneously (more on this in the next chapter) but is made to act in a certain way by feeding your past words and actions through predictive algorithms. It's meant to be an expression of your character, but the bot nonetheless appears to you as a *separate* agent. You experience it as something outside of yourself, a rival centre of consciousness rather than an extension of your own. At most you would be responsible for what it does in something like the way you might be responsible for what your child does: having been a major influence on the formation of their personality you might be responsible for them choosing the way they do, but you still didn't make the choice yourself.

Suppose the bot says something so nasty you're surprised by it. On reflection, you realize that you too might have said something equally horrid in the heat of the moment – but that you would then feel guilty for doing so. Thought experiments can be a very limited way of determining how we would respond to new technologies, but it's hard to imagine you would feel especially guilty at something a bot said on your behalf *unless* you had already come to identify with the bot in some special way that overcomes your feeling of separateness from it. In effect, to see the bot as being you, you would need to extend what philosophers sometimes call 'egocentric concern' to it. You would have to care about it in the same sort of way in which you care about yourself now.

Could you come to identify with a bot in this way, caring about it the same way you now care about yourself? Could you overcome the sense that the bot is a separate actor to yourself, a separate agent? One precondition of doing so would be that there be no other candidate for being you at the same time. Derek Parfit asks us to imagine a teleportation machine that disintegrates your body as it transmits all the data about your body and mind to Mars, where another machine uses the incoming data to build a perfect replica of you. Before you step into the teleporter, you're excited to begin your new life on Mars – that is, you identify imaginatively with the person who will step out of the teleporter at the other end. After all, that person will have your memories (including the memory of stepping into the teleporter on Earth), your personality and look exactly like you. But now suppose there's a malfunction and the machine *doesn't* disintegrate you on Earth, while still working perfectly at the other end. Now there's a person who looks and sounds just like you walking around on Mars; you can even chat to them via video link. Suddenly the replica does *not* seem to be you – precisely because, so to speak, *you* are still you. If you'd been disintegrated, the Mars person would be you by virtue of picking up where you left off; if you're still around, however, the Mars person is at best a replica and at worst an imposter.[23]

That's why, I suggest, none of the apps we've considered treat the chatbot replica that you create as being you while you're still alive. Something like Robert Nozick's 'closest continuer' theory of identity is lurking in the background here: the bot can't be you if there's a better available candidate to be you.[24] Still, not just anything can be a continuer, and it does seem inescapable that the bot won't have any first-person perspective, which will make it very hard indeed to identify with it. Transferring egocentric concern to the bot is hard to imagine, because egocentric concern is so tightly linked to being able to anticipate future experience.[25] Whatever the bot is, it isn't your *self* in our technical sense of a subjective point of view; it has no self.

But then, digital remains aren't selves in this sense either, yet I've argued these continue to present the *person* as they were. So why can't animated digital avatars continue to present the person as they were, too?

Posthumous evolution

One reason is that digital avatars, unlike 'inanimate' digital remains like social media profiles, could continue to change and evolve. Digital remains that have not been 'reanimated' stay more or less as they are. Whatever the person has written and posted at the point of death, whatever the state of their digital 'body' when they die, that is what they will be forever.

An AI-driven avatar might well be based solely on your digital remains and nothing else. But it may not stay that way: what if the process of machine learning that it initially went through to learn to speak like you continued with every interaction it undergoes? Over time, proportionally less and less of the bot's content will have come directly from the living person it is based upon. You might be training a bot now to take over from you while you die, to continue speaking on your behalf to those you leave behind, but eventually that bot will have become quite a different person from who you are now.

Ok, the bot enthusiast might reply, but that's the same as the case of a post-teleportation replica (assuming the 'original' doesn't survive): in *Star Trek*, Captain Kirk continues to have new experiences and learn new things after each time Scotty has 'beamed' him to and from the Enterprise, yet strictly speaking Kirk is in fact being destroyed and replicated over and over again. Besides, what's true in these exotic scenarios of teleportation and digital bots is true in old-fashioned organic survival too: as we go through life, we change so much over time that our future selves can seem like strangers to us. Their concerns and motivations may be so foreign to who we are now that, when we anticipate the future, we can feel as if they will be a different person altogether.[26] So the fact the bot's 'personality' will change over time, paradoxically, makes it *more* like us rather than less.

Nor will it do to insist that there's a difference between organic versus algorithmic change and learning. If the algorithms were sufficiently good, it may be that one day a bot could be built that would develop in the same way as your personality would have under the same circumstances had you lived. The bot may become crotchety and bitter with age in the same way you would have, or might mellow out just as you would have, or make exactly the unexpected late-life political shift you would have made had you lived. It might even realize it was mistaken about 'itself' while it was alive: it might, for instance, declare that it was in denial about its sexuality, or that it never in fact loved its spouse. Highly improbable, but not logically impossible.

This change in character, however, would all be happening without any subjective experience. The bot would be learning, changing, and growing, but it would not be experiencing any of that growth – or anything at all for that matter. The problem is not that the changes would not be 'true to life', but that they would be missing the first-person perspective that would allow us to identify with the bot subjectively. You can't mentally inhabit the perspective of the bot, because there *is* no perspective to inhabit. There is behaviour, but there is no consciousness.

That is also true of 'ordinary' digital remains, of course. But there's an important difference with reanimated remains. When we encounter the dead online now, the digital 'face' that we see is shot through with the consciousness that produced it, a consciousness that is nonetheless wholly gone. Recall our discussion of the photo of would-be assassin Lewis Powell: the consciousness that pierces us through the photograph is both present and long-gone. Part of what makes this paradoxical encounter possible is the very impossibility of dialogue: if the photograph of Powell were to start talking to us, we would no longer be in the presence of an absent consciousness. Instead we'd be confronted with a simulated consciousness that would replace, rather than represent, the departed. And that shifts us from metaphysical worries about whether a reanimated avatar would *be* the dead, to whether avatar-building is something we *should* do to and with the dead.

Just before we turn to ethics though, here's one further complication to think about. As Matthew Arnold and colleagues point out, scholarly discussions of digital avatars have focussed on the relationship between a single dead person and their living survivors: 'The social life of the dead, therefore, is only made social through relations with the living and not with other deceased "persons." There is no community of the dead produced in these imaginary and creative spaces of conversation. But', they ask, 'surely this need not always be so?'[27] After all, why should a digital avatar, if its governing AI is sufficiently autonomous, not start interacting with other such avatars?

We're assuming that the digital dead will behave like memories, sitting around passively waiting for us to 'activate' them. That may not be the case. If an AI was sufficiently autonomous, what's to stop it preferring the company of other bots? What happens when the bots start learning from each other? What might emerge is a form of life so alien to us that we can't recognize it as a form of *human* survival at all.

The 2017 film *Marjorie Prime* is set around the year 2050, in a time where Alzheimer's patients are given 'Prime' versions of their departed loved ones, life-size holograms who listen to their stories and then retell their life stories to them when they forget. As the story progresses, characters die and the survivors order Prime versions of those they've lost. The film ends with the Prime versions of the protagonists sitting in a room together, reminiscing about lives they never in fact lived.[28]

Replacing the dead

Defenders of digital reanimation may well reply that we're missing the point. All they're trying to do is enhance how we remember the dead, not replace them. (Quite different from, for instance, the reported trend of widowed men ordering sex dolls in the likeness of their dead wives.)[29] The creators of services like Eterni.Me insist they merely want to preserve the dead in an accessible form – which I've argued we have a duty to do. If photos made it easier to remember the dead than portraits did,[30] if video made it easier again, and if social media then made the forms of remembrance available to us richer still, why shouldn't making those profiles speak enhance memorialization even further? After all, it would preserve even more of the communicative style and depth of the person who has died.

As he got older, the philosopher Jacques Derrida often found himself asked to give eulogies for friends. Being Derrida, he spends quite a bit of these eulogies reflecting on the act of eulogizing itself, and identifies a troubling conundrum: we must speak for the dead, for they can no longer speak for themselves, yet there is something indecent about doing so. In trying to speak for the dead we end up taking over the deceased's words as one's own. '[A] certain mimetism', Derrida worries, 'is at once a duty (to take him into oneself, to identify with him in order to let him speak within oneself, to make him present and faithfully to represent him) and the worst of temptations, the most indecent and most murderous.'[31]

Digital reanimation might, at first blush, look like a neat solution to that problem. Instead of speaking on the dead's behalf, we give them the tools to speak for themselves. Like a will, which extends and enacts the agency of the testator after their death, an interactive avatar would be a sort of proxy: speaking in a way largely determined and constrained *by* the dead person herself, if also by the limitations of AI.

Even if that's true from the perspective of the dead person themselves *before* they die – and I've argued that it's not clear we could identify subjectively with proxies of this sort, given they have no conscious experience we can anticipate – things might be considerably more ethically fraught from the perspective of their survivors.

I first wrote about digital avatars, briefly, in 2011. In 2015, Buben noted that I seem 'to be a bit more optimistic about the prospects of technological preservation (of persons, if not selves, in his technical sense)' than he is.³² But in the years since, I've come to share Buben's pessimism. Let me explain his argument for why digital avatars are ethically problematic, and then add my own further concern.

Buben's critique turns on an important distinction between *recollection* and *replacement* of the dead:

> The former aims to keep us aware of what has been taken from us – it is thus in part an attempt at preservation of an irremediable void; but the latter seeks to overcome, ignore, or at least mitigate the fact that anything has been lost at all – it is an attempt at preservation of the status quo.³³

The idea of 'preserving an irremediable void' sounds paradoxical, but as we've seen, that's just the nature of how the dead appear to us: present and absent at the same time. Preserving them amounts to ensuring they retain this paradoxical state and do not become *simply* absent. Replacement makes the opposite move: it seeks to make the dead *simply* present.

Replacement, as Buben puts it, 'has little to do with the dead themselves' but is rather 'more about filling a role in someone's life which has been vacated due to a death, with something *else* capable of playing the part'.³⁴ Such a drive to replace those we've lost is understandable: we miss the dead, and in particular we miss being able to talk to them – so if we can find something that fills that void as seamlessly as possible, why wouldn't we? In Buben's scenario, if I go from talking to my organic mother to the hologram she left behind for me, what's the harm?

There are at least two, closely related, reasons why this sort of replacement is ethically troubling. Both are to do with what this technology says about our attitude to the dead themselves. Firstly, replacement reduces the dead to a mere resource for fulfilling our needs.

As Alexis Elder puts it, chatbot replacement 'treats the friend as valuable merely as a means to conversation, rather than an object worthy in its own right'.[35] Buben frames this in the language of Martin Heidegger's relatively late essay 'The Question Concerning Technology', where Heidegger complains that technological progress reduces the things of the natural world to what he calls 'standing reserve'. To see something as 'standing reserve' is to see it as its potential future instrumental use. Hence a forest becomes a forestry, an ocean becomes a fishery, a geological formation becomes a lode; trees, fish and rocks are no longer permitted to be simply what they are in themselves, but only what we can do with them and the value we can extract from them.[36]

Replacement treats the dead as just such a resource, available for manipulation and exploitation in order to benefit the living. I don't, to be clear, say that *any* such use is exploitative in this way. Just as it may be possible to lovingly tend a forest while drawing timber from it, it might be possible to lovingly tend someone's digital legacy while deploying it in new ways. But just as the tree may have an intrinsic value that means exploiting it is not *automatically* morally ok, so too treating the dead as a resource is something that still needs to be justified.

The bar for such justification will be quite high. For one thing, the dead are generally being asked to do things they never consented to, and are now permanently in a position where they are entirely at the mercy of the living. 'One is under an unconditional obligation only toward the dead', as Derrida puts it, for 'One can always negotiate conditions with the living. Upon death, there is a rupture of symmetry.'[37] This powerlessness of the dead confronts us with an ethical choice: either an openness to the dead that, as Buben puts it, 'allows the dead to show up in some sense as they were', or exploitation and manipulation to suit our own purposes.[38] The ethical point here is roughly a Kantian one: we wrong the dead when we treat them as a means to our own ends instead of ends in themselves.

But what about Buben's scenario where his mother, far from being an unwitting participant, helps to build the avatar while she's alive? Or what of an actor who explicitly consents to their image being reused after they die, in ways they cannot now anticipate? In such cases we might even violate the interests of the dead by *not* reanimating them. Even if the dead did consent while alive, however, that does not automatically make exploiting them as a resource permissible. Some uses would still be degrading, inconsistent with the beliefs or values of the dead, or otherwise antithetical to what we might take their interests to be. There's also the problem that these are presumably open-ended agreements: users of services like Eterni.Me aren't asking that their bots be shut down one hundred years from now. The idea that someone can irreversibly sign away rights over themselves, which is already a highly contentious point among liberal political theorists, looks even more troubling when not even death can terminate the arrangement. Once again, we simply don't yet have social, let alone legal, norms to guide us here.

Reducing the dead to resources for the living is bad enough. But here's my second, related concern: treating the dead as replaceable also degrades the *living*, pre-mortem person. To assume that an AI avatar can take up where a dead person left off in fulfilling certain functions in my life is to treat the person we're mourning as if they were a fungible good all along,[39] something we could have swapped out for a replacement without too much loss. That perverts the very impulse which leads us to recollect the dead in the first place: the uniqueness of the person who we seek to 'rescue from insignificance'. Part of the pathos of loss is our pained awareness of the very *ir*replaceability of the dead, the fact that it is *this* person in her distinctive otherness who I love and who is now both radically absent and yet persistent. That distinctiveness is essential to that sense of absence. Lewis' *A Grief Observed* distils this dry philosophical point into an articulate howl of pain:

> What pitiable cant to say 'She will live forever in my memory'! *Live?* That is exactly what she won't do. You might as well think like the old Egyptians that you can keep the dead by embalming them. Will nothing persuade us that they are gone? What's left? A corpse, a memory, and (in some versions) a ghost. All mockeries or horrors. Three more ways of spelling the word *dead*. It was H I loved. As if I wanted to fall in love with my memory of her, an image in my own mind! It would be a sort of incest.[40]

And yet, 'H' (the writer Joy Davidman, who died at the age of just 45) *is* very much present in Lewis' grief: 'she seems to meet me everywhere', not as an apparition but as something that remains 'momentously real' or 'obstinately real', 'a sort of unobtrusive but massive sense that she is, just as much as ever, a fact to be taken into account'.[41]

To replace the irreplaceable is to concede it was never in fact irreplaceable at all. It implies you don't love *this* person but whoever or whatever turns up to fulfil certain roles they play in your life. The memorialized social network profile preserves the dead, though in a reduced form, while the avatar, in replacing the dead, degrades the dead *and* the living by treating them as replaceable. A perhaps ill-advised analogy: if a memorialized online profile is like a taxidermied pet, an avatar of the dead is like buying a new pet of the same breed and giving it the same name as the old one.

To be absolutely clear, I don't believe anyone who has set up these avatars to date sees them as replacing the dead. As the moving cases of Roman Mazurenko and Jang Nayeon demonstrate, these technologies so far have been focused on remembrance and assisting in mourning, not offering a substitute for those that have been lost.

It's quite possible, as Elder argues by drawing on classical Confucian texts about ritual in mourning, that a judicious use of avatars of the dead could be beneficial for managing grief.[42] Technologies are only as good or bad as the use we make of them. But recall how quickly we adapt to technology: just a century separates us from Forster's 'I hear something like you through this telephone, but I do not hear you.' Could we really slip into a way of engaging with avatars that treats them as replacements for the dead? It might be better to ask, what's to stop us?

Faithfulness to the concrete singularity of the dead demands we recollect the dead, but to recollect them also *as dead*, as lost to us even if still with us in various ways. We now have technology that makes it easier to do the first part. Our digital memories maintain the dead among the living better than ever. The risk now is that the technology will make it harder to do the second part. In remembering the dead more effectively we may end up forgetting, in effect, that they are dead.

At this point, we reach the end of what existing technology is capable of. In the final chapter, we turn to a chilling piece of speculative fiction, where we find a warning of the traps that await us – and, perhaps, a hint as to how we might yet escape.

7

Prey to the living

The British comedian and TV presenter Charlie Brooker's *Black Mirror* series has provided some of the most disturbing television of the last decade. In the tradition of *The Twilight Zone*, each episode is a self-contained story, generally set in a near-future world yet not-so-subtly interrogating our present-day relationship to technology; the title 'black mirror' refers to what you're left with when you turn off a screen.

Among researchers working on digital death, one episode in particular has sparked enormous discussion – so much so that it's almost hackneyed now to discuss it. Yet 'Be Right Back', the 2013 second season opener, is worth dwelling on a little longer.[1] By pushing just a bit further than the digital resurrection technologies that were already being contemplated at the time, the episode shows up the risks involved in this new relationship to the dead, and gestures to where salvation might come from.

Be Right Back

In 'Be Right Back' we are introduced to a couple, Martha (Hayley Atwell) and Ash (Domhnall Gleeson) who have just moved to a house in the countryside. The next day, Ash goes to return the moving van they've rented, and, in circumstances that aren't shown, is killed.

At Ash's funeral, Martha's friend Sarah tells her about a new service, 'still in beta', that Sarah found helpful in getting through her grief in a similar situation. Martha refuses, but Sarah signs her up for the service anyway. The service scrapes Ash's online footprint and builds it into a text-based chat bot (remember, this episode aired two years before Roman Mazurenko died). There's an interesting moment where Sarah tells Martha 'I know he's dead, but it wouldn't work if he wasn't' – it seems you can only relate to these bots as a replacement if there is, to return to Nozick's term, no 'closer continuer' left.

Though reluctant at first, Martha finds herself interacting more and more with the chatbot. The bot, it turns out, is quite good at upselling, and suggests Martha upgrade to the next level the service offers. By uploading audio and video recordings of Ash, the service is able to give the chatbot synthesized speech that sounds indistinguishable from the living Ash's voice. Now Martha can speak to Ash as though talking to him on the phone. She chats freely and cheerfully to him on long walks, while avoiding her very-much-alive sister's phone calls. In the middle of all this, Martha discovers she's pregnant.

Finally, Martha upgrades to the premium level of service. An inert, mannequin-like body is delivered to her house. Martha then follows the Ash-bot's instructions, putting the body in a bath with water and electrolytes to activate it. In due course, a completely lifelike clone of Ash emerges from the bath, covered in realistic-feeling synthetic skin. The literary allusion is hard to miss; as Tama Leaver puts it, 'Ash is, in many respects, a social media version of Frankenstein's monster, not violent, but nevertheless disrupting the everyday norms and boundaries of life'.[2]

This version of Ash sounds, feels, and looks like the organic Ash, though it is not an organism. It can eat, but it doesn't actually need to;

it can close its eyes at night if asked to do so, but it does not need to sleep. When injured, its synthetic skin heals immediately. Because the replica Ash is based on photos, videos and social media posts, it is a somewhat idealized version of the original: when Martha comments that the automaton looks like Ash on one of his better days, he replies 'The photos we keep tend to be flattering. I guess I wasn't any different.'

That phrasing should raise alarm. Who's 'I'? Why 'was'? Yet Martha pushes through her unease and surrenders to the sense of continuity. 'I missed you', she tells the clone. 'I missed you so much.'

Speaking and forgetting

We've already mentioned both Jacques Derrida and C.S. Lewis – two species that don't tend to meet in the wild, so to speak. In their very different ways, the French deconstructionist philosopher and the British novelist and theologian both found themselves grappling with the threat of replacing the dead. Both worried that out of love for the dead, we can end up obliterating them in the very attempt to preserve them.

In his eulogies, Derrida wrestled with how to speak *for* the dead without speaking *instead* of them. Derrida maintains that the dead 'can no longer be but *in us*',[3] and takes this being-in-us seriously; yet he also insists that 'nothing can begin to dissipate the terrifying and chilling light of this certainty' that the one dead 'is no more, he is no longer here, no longer there',[4] that 'our friend [is] gone forever, irremediably absent [...] for it would be unfaithful to delude oneself into believing that the other living *in us* is living *in himself*.'[5]

Frankly, this all feels a bit abstract and arcane for a eulogy. But you can see Derrida wrestling with a real, living problem here: he must speak the truth that is his friend, yet his friend is gone. He must speak for the dead, yet doing so risks replacing his friend with Derrida's own version of him.

Early in his own grief, Lewis too begins to worry that in trying to remember his recently dead wife he was in fact replacing her with his own fictionalized version of her. The version of H living inside, to borrow Derrida's language, is necessarily filtered through the quirks and biases of Lewis' own psychology. The longer this goes on, Lewis worries, the more he will begin to supplant H with a fiction of his own unwitting and unwilling creation. The fictitious H, the image Lewis builds up of her in his mind, comes to take over precisely because 'The reality is no longer there to check me, to pull me up short, as the real H so often did, so unexpectedly, by being so thoroughly herself and not me.'[6] Deprived of the 'rough, sharp, cleansing tang of her otherness,'[7] which would instantly wash this imposter away, Lewis is thrown back on memories and ideas about H which are increasingly a reflection of himself.

Worse, Lewis worries that this falsified version of H would come to function as a tool for achieving his own ends: 'I should soon be using "what H. would have liked" as an instrument of domestic tyranny; with her supposed likings becoming a thinner and thinner disguise for my own.'[8] In speaking for the dead, we can end up speaking on behalf of a version of the dead that is really a creature of our own desires and interests. 'It's what she would have wanted' becomes a way of getting what *we* want.

As we've already noted, 'overwrite' is a risk in online memorialization in general, and as Lewis' snowflakes analogy and Derrida's eulogy anxieties suggest, this technological risk mirrors one built into organic memory. Every act of remembering is itself a reconstruction of the past, a new *event* of recreating what has happened and thereby connecting with past events. It may just be that we're stuck with this, that we overwrite the dead that little bit every time we think of them – whether that's in our heads or on the screen.

One way to understand this overwrite is to think of it as a forgetting or covering-over of the absence of the dead – in effect, forgetting the *death* of the dead. The danger is that we generate a seductive image of the dead for ourselves, and then confuse that image for the actual person who has died.

Fatal obedience

So, what has this got to do with digital avatars of the dead? Well, consider Ash: the Ash-clone is, as any such AI-driven avatar must be, a collection of algorithms that embed statistical likelihoods based on past behaviour. He can't really do anything truly *new*, but can only act in a sort of subjunctive way: just as we guess what someone *would have* said based on what they *used to* say, Ash is ultimately just doing what Ash *would have* done when exposed to novel situations and new information. His actions are a projection of the past into the present.

That's a serious limitation of any online avatar for at least two reasons. The first is that the avatar can only ever be as good as the predictive algorithm that governs it. Many of us have had the experience of holding a conversation with a dead person in our heads,[9] applying a sort of tacit algorithm to give us, at best, a somewhat self-conscious guess about what they would have said had they been here. Recalling Michel Foucault, Derrida says 'This is one of the questions that I would have liked to ask him. I am trying, since this is, unfortunately, the only recourse left us in the solitude of questioning, to imagine the principle of the reply.'[10] Sometimes, sadly, we just won't be able to imagine such a principle – and nor will those constructing an avatar.

Secondly, this means that in some sense the words we hear from an avatar of the dead are not really coming from the dead person at all. When we imagine talking to a person who has died, we continually run up against what Jean-Paul Sartre called the 'essential poverty' of a mental image, the fact that 'nothing can be learned from an image that is not already known'.[11] Try this little test: in Edvard Munch's iconic painting 'The Scream', how many boats are on the water? You can't get the answer just by calling up the image of the painting in your mind, because in a sense you're *putting* however many boats there are into the picture yourself. Google the image, however, and you'll see details that exist independently of your mind that you can check. (Two boats, in case the suspense is too much for you.)

This same problem applies to any attempt to reanimate the dead. What comes 'from' the dead in our imagination of what they would say or do ultimately comes from us, not them. What we put into the mouth of the dead, however well-informed our guess might be, is in some sense counterfeit. Lewis realizes this too. Our image of the dead, says Lewis,

> has the added disadvantage that it will do whatever you want. It will smile or frown, be tender, gay, ribald, or argumentative just as your mood demands. It is a puppet of which you hold the strings. [...] the fatal obedience of the image, its insipid dependence on me, is bound to increase.[12]

This 'fatal obedience' is precisely why the dead are so vulnerable to being warped into serving our interests ('He would have wanted me to have this'), but it also greatly dampens whatever jolt of recognition we can get from the dead, at least from our own imagination. Being struck by the distinctive way a person is in the world is a large part of how we relate to others as individual, loveable people, and this is true of the dead too. We want that moment of 'ah, that's just what she'd say!' – yet that shock of recognition isn't available when we remember or reconstruct the dead, because *we* supply the words the dead speak. Uncalculated, spontaneous communications from the dead cannot happen in our imagination because on some level we've chosen for them what they will say.

Ordinarily, when we find ourselves holding a conversation with a dead person in our head, the experience is pervaded with this awareness that the dead are simply parroting what we 'give' them to say. The dead, in that respect at least, are not unlike fictional characters, who may speak according to their own internal logic (which is why it makes sense for an actor to object 'but my character would never say that!'), but ultimately only say and do what their creators tell them to.

An avatar, however, is something outside of us. Yes, it is driven by algorithms that try to predict what the dead *would have* said, just as our own imagination of the dead tries to do. The algorithm can't, in an important sense, produce anything that wasn't already sitting there waiting to be activated, just as a mental image or a fictional character can't contain anything we didn't put there. But faced with such an avatar, we won't have the same direct awareness of this as we do in imagination.

On the level of our lived experience, then, the avatar reopens that risk of telic possibility we've seen recur several times. Just as the mourners of Jack Froese could accept emails as if they *might as well have* come from their dead friend, it would be very easy to slip into viewing an avatar of the dead as if its words *might as well be* those of the deceased, so long as we can't see the algorithms at work. Friends of Roman Mazurenko said his bot sounds very much like him: it's possible to have a 'that's just the sort of thing he'd say!' moment because the words seem to be coming not from our own imagination but from something outside ourselves.

This all suggests that replacement, rather than recollection, is a worryingly real possibility. For an AI avatar of the dead to function as replacement would involve forgetting that the words are being arranged by a non-conscious piece of software, that everything it says is merely the result of running things our friend once said through a series of complex rules. Such forgetting would be akin to the 'epistemic failure' model of telepresence: our friend appears to be here with us just so long as we can't see the mechanics of how the words are made.

Is such forgetting a genuine risk? It's hard to see why it wouldn't be. The whole trajectory of electronic communication from Morse onwards is towards an instantaneousness that allows for the experience of direct, synchronous co-presence. We become so embodied to our media that we no longer even notice *that* they are media, that our words are mediated; why, then, would we not become so used to avatars of the dead that we accept and treat them as if they're the dead themselves?

Alterity

If this is something we want to keep from happening, there's hope to be found in just that capacity of other people to surprise, confuse or confound us. Our salvation from replacement might ultimately come down to the *alterity*, or otherness, of other people.

Alterity is one of those words that gets used quite loosely in different academic disciplines, but among continental philosophers it's been most usefully applied to the dimension of other people that sets them apart from both ourselves and from all the other objects we encounter and interact with, that unknowable inner life of others. The term has been theorized by different thinkers for quite different purposes, but for the present discussion think of Emmanuel Levinas' description of how the face of the other breaks into my otherwise self-contained world.[13] Or think of Sartre's description of the effect of realizing there is another person in the park where I am standing: where until just now I saw the park as a field of objects converging on me, suddenly I see the whole world rearranged towards the other.[14] That the thing sitting on the park bench over there is not a *mere* thing, but another consciousness, another – rival – point of view on the world, changes my whole experience of the park itself. I can see the things you see, but I can never see them through your eyes – and you will always exceed any perceptions or judgments I might make of you. Alterity is the fact that there is always more to another person than can ever meet the eye.

The alterity of the dead is, as Derrida notes, a sort of *alterity of alterity*; death makes the other even more remote and separate from us than they were in life:

> The one who looks at us in us – and *for whom* we are – is no longer; he is completely other, infinitely other, as he has always been, and death has more than ever entrusted him, given him over, distanced him, in this infinite alterity.[15]

> If the relation to the other presupposes an infinite separation, an infinite interruption where the face appears, what happens, where and to whom does it happen, when another interruption comes at death to hollow out even more infinitely this first separation, a rending interruption at the heart of interruption itself?[16]

The 'world' of the other, their interiority from which we were already at one remove while they lived, is doubly lost to us; it 'sinks into an abyss from which no memory – even if we keep the memory, and we will keep it – can save it'.[17]

We might think that the dead, being permanently deprived of consciousness, would lose their alterity, and fall back into the world of inert objects. What was once a living, breathing person is now just a lump of organic matter. As we've seen though, that is not what happens. The corpse continues to present the face, and manages to both be and not-be the person who has died. The face remains as the seat of a consciousnesses that *has been*, a consciousness lost to the world and yet which continues to haunt it.

Yet the otherness of the dead remains fragile and easily overwhelmed. Derrida claims the abundance of the other 'makes it incumbent upon us not to totalize or simplify, not to immobilize him or fix a trajectory [...] not to take hold of what was inappropriable and must remain so'.[18] In other words: don't treat a person (dead or otherwise!) as something that can be wholly known, and so wholly predicted. In remembering the dead we need to respect the person's otherness, including their ability to surprise or confound us. Lewis, dealing with the death of H, notes this same alterity, along with the way it defeats our attempts at appropriation, and that it is *this* alterity that we are to love in the dead:

> All reality is iconoclastic. The earthly beloved, even in this life, incessantly triumphs over your mere idea of her. And you want her to; you want her with all her resistances, all her faults, all her unexpectedness. That is, in her foursquare and independent reality. And this, not any image or memory, is what we are to love still, after she is dead.[19]

Derrida, for his part, is not wholly convinced that alterity can be completely lost by the dead:

> Living, Roland Barthes cannot be reduced to that which each or all of us can think, believe, know, and already recall of him. But

once dead, might he not be so reduced? No, but the chances of the illusion will be greater *and* lesser, other in any case.[20]

To replace the dead, in Buben's sense, is to do just this, to reduce the dead to what we know of them and treat them as resources for the living. Derrida seems to think however that the alterity of the dead, the way in which they always outstrip our memories and recollections of them just as the living outstrip whatever we can see and think of them, provides some defence against this possibility.

Fascinatingly, that's exactly how things come to grief in 'Be Right Back'. Martha's life with the replica Ash begins to sour, but not because of the clone's differences from the original Ash. Because Ash's sexual responses were never recorded while he lived, the avatar can't respond sexually in the distinctive way Ash would have done; instead, having learned its sexual technique from online porn videos, it is capable of providing more vigorous lovemaking than the original Ash could. When cut, its skin heals instantly, and it feels no pain. These differences, though striking, aren't a deal-breaker for Martha.

What *does* bring Martha's relationship with the avatar to a crisis point is the clone's lack of those 'resistances, faults, and unexpectedness' that Lewis describes. The clone is just too pliable. It meekly complies whenever it is told to do something – even in situations where Ash would have resisted or refused. At one point, Martha actually begs the clone to fight her, becoming more and more frustrated at his lack of resistance, his failure to, literally and metaphorically, push back. The clone asks Martha in response if Ash ever hit her. No, she replies, of course not, but he might have done had she struck him the way Martha is hitting the clone now. It's every bit as unsettling as it sounds.

The clone is a clever replica, but in one sense it is *too* much like Ash as he was: its every move is determined by algorithmic processes working on how Ash acted in the past. There is no spontaneity in the clone, no genuine originality, no *genius* in Schopenhauer's sense. If Kierkegaard is right that the dead cannot coerce or cajole us, nor it seems can they really surprise us, even in this reanimated form.[21]

In 2018 a type of AI known as a generative adversarial network, which had been trained on 15,000 portraits from various eras, created a portrait of a man entitled 'Edmond de Bellamy'. Initially valued at US$7,000–10,000, the painting instead reached an eye-watering $432,500 at auction at Christies in New York.[22] It's hard not to be both impressed and disturbed by this machine incursion into human creativity. But perhaps we should hold our applause a little longer. Nikolaus Lehner makes the point that such an algorithm may one day be able to produce an artwork that looks impressively convincing as the sort of painting Caravaggio, for instance, would produce. But something would still be missing: 'the genius and the humane [*sic*] of the original Caravaggio are likely not to be found in the self-reproduction of a structure but in the very transgression of himself as a communicative structure'.[23] In other words, Caravaggio is not just a painter who produces paintings that look like Caravaggios; he is a painter able to go beyond Caravaggio and still be Caravaggio. What is true of Caravaggio here is true of everyone: part of someone's distinctive way of being is their capacity to take us by surprise while still being *them*. Spontaneity is crucial: 'In a particular sense', adds Lehner, 'to be predictable means to be dead'. What really troubles us about algorithms, whether they're generating poetry or suggesting products we might like to buy on Amazon, is that they suggest we too are predictable, calculable – somehow already dead.[24]

In the end, Martha concludes the Ash clone cannot take Ash's place: 'You're just a performance of stuff that he performed without thinking and it's not enough!' Martha takes 'Ash' to a cliff-top and orders him to jump off. He moves to comply. There is, after all, no consciousness going on here, and so no fear, let alone fear of death. Martha points out that the real Ash would not have accepted his fate so quietly. He would have been scared – whereupon the clone starts begging for its life. 'No, that's not fair' says Martha, as the weeping clone pleads that it doesn't want to die. Martha screams. Cut to black.

For all its bleakness, 'Be Right Back' is, at least up until its epilogue, touchingly optimistic: it implies that there's something in human consciousness that simply can't be captured in algorithms. The Ash avatar fails because the interiority and spontaneity of the original Ash aren't genuinely available to it; his individuality exceeds and resists capture in AI form. There's a hope here that alterity might finally override and defeat our algorithmic replacements. What separates human from avatar is that spark of something free and perpetually new – the light in the faces of others.

That assumption may turn out to be hopelessly naive. It may well be that our whole experience of people, of alterity and spontaneity, rests upon a set of biological facts that are at base completely determined. If that's so, then the impediments to building a fully convincing avatar are merely technical and contingent. It's not just that an avatar of the dead might pass a Turing Test one day, or that CGI might become indistinguishable from live-action film, but that such an avatar might also learn to push back, to surprise, to perform otherness in a way that we would find indistinguishable from the real thing.

The epilogue to 'Be Right Back' takes place several years later. It's Martha's daughter's birthday. She has a birthday cake, and gives a slice to Martha, takes one for herself – and another slice to take 'upstairs'. 'It's not the weekend', objects Martha. 'But it is my birthday', says the girl. She takes the third slice up to the attic and gives it to the Ash clone, now 'living' silently and motionlessly in the attic until visited. 'I brought you some cake', the girl declares. 'I know you don't eat anything, I'm just using you as an excuse so I can get an extra slice.' 'Devious!' says Ash. The girl calls Martha up to join them.

I fear the epilogue is right. Trusting in the spontaneity and uniqueness of each person might not be enough to overcome our tendency to get used to new media. When the replicas come, we might eventually shrug and come to accept them. They won't be perfect, but they might be good enough to keep in the attic to eat cake with, as it were. And that does not just dishonour the dead; it volatilizes our entire relationship to the living as well.

A modest proposal: meet the glitch

Don Ihde once noted that when it comes to new technology, philosophers always turn up too late to the party. We're rarely part of the R&D phase, and are instead wheeled out to provide philosophical and ethical guidance once the technologies are already deployed, or at least well advanced. The assumption is always that if a new technology *can* do something, it *will* be used to do that thing regardless, and philosophers are brought in to triage the resulting ethical casualties: 'For applied ethics in this context, it is always after the technologies are in place that the ambulance corps arrives.'[25] Unsurprising, then, that we find ourselves with our digital replacements already waiting in the wings and little discussion of whether this is something we should allow at all, or under what conditions or restraints.

It seems deeply unlikely that philosophers are going to stop these technologies, if indeed anyone can. Even so, I want to offer a suggestion.

The saving grace of avatar technologies up to this point is that they simply haven't been good enough. There is always something to remind us that we're not dealing with a living person, whether that's stilted or incoherent responses or unconvincing or un-lifelike visual features. Something always gets in the way and so calls attention to the simulated nature of what we're doing. Alexis Elder has argued that in building chatbots of the dead that could be used ethically for healthy mourning, 'it seems important that developers not aim for photorealism, or for bots that would pass the Turing test' to avoid the risk of replacing the dead with avatars.[26] But Elder herself notes that bots don't need to be entirely convincing to elicit emotional reactions from people,[27] and in any case, with the rise of technology like deepfakes, it seems increasingly unlikely that chatbots will remain unconvincing for much longer.

It may be, however, that we can build a different kind of deficiency into these technologies. Buben invokes Heidegger to frame his (justified) worry about reducing the dead to resources for the living. Heidegger might also provide the answer for what we should do here, too. In a famous passage in *Being and Time*, Heidegger explores what it is to encounter something as *ready-to-hand* using the now-clichéd example of a hammer. So long as the hammer works, we don't even think about it as an object; we just drive in nails, absorbed in our work. It's only when the hammer breaks, becoming 'unready-to-hand', that it calls attention to itself as a physical thing.[28]

Much of our media technology follows exactly this phenomenology. You don't notice you're holding a phone up to your ear and listening to an electronically reconstructed version of someone's voice *until* the call drops out or the battery dies. When we become engrossed in something on a screen, the screen itself and all the technology behind it falls away from our awareness, unless something goes wrong to draw our attention back to it. Glitches break our absorption and break the spell. Perhaps, then, glitches can stop us becoming so engrossed in talking to an avatar that we slip into treating it as a real person.

In other words, if we are to have AI avatars of the dead, we should compel those who create them to build in deliberate glitches. We have become remarkably good at making our telecommunications transparent, having to deal less and less with disruptions that break our flow. Here, however, we perhaps have good reason to preserve the disruptions instead of trying to weed them out. Building in bugs that remind us of the simulated nature of the person with whom we are dealing, with their absence of genuine subjectivity, would allow us to resist using the dead as replaceable resources. It would help us to recall their lostness. If these avatars periodically become 'unready-to-hand', it might just provide enough friction to make it clear to us that the dead, though still with us, are also gone.

It's most unlikely this will ever happen, of course, and hard to say just how effective it would be if it did. Still, we need new norms for dealing with the digital dead, and those norms may not be at all what we expect them to be. 'Make your bots buggy' is certainly not a norm we could have foreseen, but it may well be one we need.

'To be dead', said Sartre, 'is to be a prey for the living'.[29] The dead are at our mercy, not least because they depend on us, the living, to save them from oblivion. Everything tends towards entropy, towards forgetting. In a very short space of time we have, largely by accident, given the dead new ways to survive, new ways to present themselves before the living. By building an enormous electronic infrastructure that remembers everything by default, we have successfully tipped the scales away from forgetting, from absence. Perhaps we're at least smart enough to stop things slipping too far the other way. The challenge is, in a sense, just what it always was: to not forget the dead, but not forget the dead *are* dead.

Coda: Mind uploads?

We've now come to the end of our discussion of whether and how we can survive death through the internet. At this point, you may well feel a bit cheated: surely we're just getting started? Why are we stopping at memorialized profiles and digital avatars? What about the far more exciting prospect of uploading our minds into computer networks?

Indeed, in his book *Internet Afterlife*, the philosopher Kevin O'Neill is dismissive of the sorts of online immortality we've been discussing up to this point, but insists that mind uploading really would count as digital survival of death.[1] Plenty of transhumanists agree: if we could find some way to transfer our minds into computers, then we would finally shed the vulnerabilities of the flesh. We could live as long as there are networks to sustain us (and, presumably, workers to sustain those networks). Even better, because it's our minds that have been uploaded, not just records of words and pictures we've left behind, we'd get to *experience* this form of survival.

Various groups claim to be actively working towards this goal. In particular, the Terasem Foundation, a transhumanist movement founded by entrepreneur and lawyer Martine Rothblatt, has been especially prominent. Through a project called 'Lifenaut', Terasem claims to give people the opportunity 'to create a digital back-up of their mind and genetic code'.[2] As with some of the other services we've looked at, users are invited to set up and train an avatar based on their 'MindFile' (a database of personal reflections captured in video, image, audio and documents about yourself). But whereas Enterni.Me and others claim they're not setting up a replacement of the dead, Lifenaut explicitly aims – long term! – to use these 'digital back-ups' of people's minds and DNA to effect 'the transfer of human consciousness to computers/robots and beyond'. In particular, the backup of the mind would be used to develop a 'Mindclone':

> Mindclones are self-aware digital beings, able to think, reason, remember, and feel. A mindclone would be functionally identical to the living biological original mind simply existing now in two different substrates, one digital and one flesh. Your mindclone and you will cast the same vote, love the same children, and receive the same jury duty summons, and when your physical body dies you will live on, forever, as your mindclone.[3]

Once again, the idea has been explored more compellingly in fiction – and once again, we turn to *Black Mirror*. In 'San Junipero' (2016), we witness the beginning of a romantic relationship between Yorkie (Mackenzie Davis) and Kelly (Gugu Mbatha-Raw) in the resort town of San Junipero in 1987.[4] We eventually learn that this town is in fact a computer simulation, where the elderly can re-experience life in their youthful bodies. The offline Yorkie has been paralysed since the age of twenty-one, and wants to be euthanized so she can live in San Junipero permanently. In other words, this is a future in which we can enter virtual worlds before we die, and then have our minds persist in those worlds, having the same experiences, after our physical bodies die.

Tama Leaver notes that compared to 'Be Right Back', 'San Junipero' is less interested in the mechanics of how this form of digital survival might work.[5] Fiction, of course, doesn't necessarily need to explain such things to help us explore what such a world might be like. Yet the problems remain, and they are not merely practical.

Technologically, we are no doubt a very long way from any of this ever happening, or even from understanding what it would be to copy the information that makes someone the person they are from a brain into an electronic format. We don't even understand how consciousness arises from the brain (the infamous 'Hard Problem')[6] let alone how to take it out of a brain and into a different medium. Philosophers have also doubted whether mind-uploading, were it possible, would produce a life worth living. Christine Overall for instance accepts that computers might make certain kinds of self-memorialization possible, but insists that 'Containment within a computer hardly provides the kinds of opportunities for ongoing human experience and activity that are associated with being a person.'[7]

But there's a deeper problem for this sort of technology, if it's meant to produce robust, live-on-in-my-apartment-style, first-person survival. For that sort of survival to happen, we have to be able to experience it. I cannot look forward to life as a non-conscious computer program that sounds just like me, any more than I can look forward to being a chatbot. But let's imagine that we could somehow overcome that problem and give the computer program subjectivity.[8] We'd still be missing one more element: not only must the computer program be conscious, it must be the *same* consciousness as the one we have now. (Just as it's not enough that my teleporter replica on Mars has the same *type* of consciousness as me: for me to be justified in anticipating his experiences, his consciousness must be one and the same as the consciousness I have now.)

The problem is that we simply don't know what it would be for a first-person perspective to move from one substrate (a brain) to another (a computer) and yet be the same first-person perspective. Indeed, as I've argued elsewhere, serious conceptual problems emerge as soon as we try re-identifying first-person perspectives at different times at all. It's a sort of category mistake, in which we treat something that's irreducibly present tense as if it's an object that can also exist yesterday or tomorrow.[9] So if I'm told that I'm about to die, but that at the moment of my death my Lifenaut Mindclone will be activated, it's still far from clear I can take comfort in that prospect. I know that *a* consciousness will exist at that moment, finishing the thought I'd just begun at the moment of death. But is that *my* consciousness? Is *his* self *my* self? It's not even clear that this is a coherent question, let alone one we can answer in the affirmative.

In other words, mind uploading, were it ever possible, might be a more richly detailed form of replication, but it doesn't appear to be any more of a pathway to first-personal survival than living on via a digital avatar.

But who knows. Perhaps one day we'll be so embodied to these sorts of technologies that we will indeed come to identify with our Mindclones so much we'll start looking forward to their experiences, coherently or not. Perhaps we'll blame the Mindclones of the long dead for the things they did in life, or gratefully pamper the Mindclones of those who died heroically. Perhaps. For now, we find ourselves at a very particular moment. The dead are dwelling amongst us more richly than before, yet they remain our dependants and our prey. We are haunted by ghosts we must choose to sustain, but not so as to rob them of their ghostliness. It turns out the real challenge of internet immortality is not to vanquish death, but to love the dead as dead.

Notes

Introduction

1 David Oderberg, 'Disembodied Communication and Religious Experience: The Online Model', *Philosophy and Technology* 25, no. 3 (2012): 382.
2 In formal terms: 'It is telically possible for S that p for purpose T in circumstances C $=_{df}$ it does not matter to S whether p for purpose T in circumstances C.' Oderberg, 'Disembodied Communication and Religious Experience', 384.
3 There were a number of news items covering the Froese emails around mid-March 2012. The source for all of these (and for the quotes above) appears to be a report by Matt Danzico, 'Emails from Dead Man's Account Spook Loved Ones', *BBC News*, 13 March 2012, https://www.bbc.com/news/av/magazine-17348635/emails-from-dead-man-s-account-spook-loved-ones, accessed 25 March 2020. Both press coverage and online obituaries spell his name 'Froese'.
4 Susan Lepselter, *The Resonance of Unseen Things: Poetics, Power, Captivity, and UFOs in the American Uncanny* (Ann Arbor, MI: University of Michigan Press, 2016), 16.
5 Owen Davies, *The Haunted: A Social History of Ghosts* (Houndsmills: Palgrave, 2007), 38–42.
6 Jeffrey Sconce, *Haunted Media: Electronic Presence from Telegraphy to Television* (Durham, NC: Duke University Press, 2000).
7 Ibid., 36.
8 Patrick Stokes, 'The Science of the Dead: Proto-spiritualism in Kierkegaard's Copenhagen', in *Kierkegaard and the Religious Crisis of the 19th Century* (*Acta Kierkegaardiana vol. 4*), ed. Roman Kralik, Abraham H. Khan, Peter Sajda, Jamie Turnbull and Andrew Burgess (Toronto and Sala: Kierkegaard Circle, 2009), 132–49.

9   Mensa Mobilis 'Et Par Ord Endnu om Borddands og Bankeaander' (Copenhagen: H.P. Møller, 1853), 2, my translation.
10 Anonymous, 'Fortællinger og Oplysninger om den Mærkværdige Nys Opfudne Borddands' (Copenhagen, 1853), 3, my translation and emphasis.
11 Ibid., 4.
12 Mobilis 'Et Par Ord Endnu om Borddands og Bankeaander', 4–5.
13 Dr Practicus, 'Borddandsen. Praktiske Raad Nedskrevne for at Gjøre det Vidunderlige Phænomen Letfatteligt og Udførligt for Enhver' (Copenhagen: B. Bro, 1853), 4–6, my translation. There's a noticeable sexual subtext in play here too. One pamphleteer passes on a claim from an American correspondent, 'Dr. R. Andræ', that mixed-gender sitters were said to produce the best results (Anonymous, 'Fortællinger og Oplysninger', 13–14), while 'Dr Practicus' recommends sitters be arranged in alternating genders, 'for the electricity more easily insinuate[s] itself from man to woman than from man to man, or woman to woman' (Practicus, 'Borddandsen', 6).
14 Laura Otis, *Networking: Communicating with Bodies and Machines in the Nineteenth Century* (Ann Arbor, MI: University of Michigan Press, 2001), 128–9; Sconce, *Haunted Media*, 34–5.
15 The poem itself first appeared in 1855 in the first edition of *Leaves of Grass*, but with neither title nor the opening line.
16 On the life of Morse see e.g. Kenneth Silverman, *Lightning Man: The Accursed Life of Samuel FB Morse* (New York: Knopf Group, 2010).
17 A.S. Rothman, 'Mr. Edison's "Life Units:" Hundred Trillion in Human Body May Scatter After Death – Machine to Register Them', *New York Times*, 23 January 1921, 1, 6.
18 Anthony Enns, 'Voices of the Dead: Transmission/translation/transgression', *Culture, Theory and Critique* 46, no. 1 (2005): 18.
19 Ibid.; Michael Arnold, Tamara Kohn, Martin Gibbs, James Meese and Bjorn Nansen, *Death and Digital Media* (London: Routledge, 2018), 20–1.
20 Tony Walter, 'Communication Media and the Dead: From the Stone Age to Facebook', *Mortality* 20, no. 3 (2015): 224. However, other sources suggest Nipper used to listen attentively to his *live* human's voice. Nipper was in any case himself dead at the time the original painting was made. See Robb Fritz, 'His Master's Voice', *McSweeney's Internet Tendency*, 27 June 2012, https://www.mcsweeneys.net/articles/his-masters-voice, accessed 26 March 2020.
21 After his initial experiments, Jürgenson actually continued to hear voices in ordinary sounds, such as rain, when *not* using a recording device (Enns, 'Voices of the Dead', 22). This strengthens the likelihood that his 'voices' were simply auditory pareidolia – pseudo-patterns heard in random noise

which seems evident from the strained and over-interpreted character of EVP 'messages' in general.
22 This story is often repeated in books about the paranormal but I have not been able to find a source for it.
23 Miki Meek, 'Really Long Distance', *This American Life*, National Public Radio, 23 September 2016, https://www.thisamericanlife.org/597/one-last-thing-before-i-go, accessed 23 April 2020. Elaine Kasket discusses the Wind Telephone in the context of digital death in her *All The Ghosts in the Machine: Illusions of Immortality in the Digital Age* (London: Robinson, 2019).
24 Kendall L. Walton, *Mimesis as Make-Believe: On the Foundations of the Representational Arts* (Cambridge, MA: Harvard University Press, 1990); 'Metaphor and Prop Oriented Make-Believe', *European Journal of Philosophy* 1, no. 1 (1993): 39–57.
25 Nora McInerny Purmort, 'Please Don't Ask Me to Put Down My Phone', *Slate*, 24 May 2016, https://slate.com/human-interest/2016/05/my-phone-is-a-time-machine-to-where-my-husband-is-still-alive.html, accessed 23 April 2020.
26 Alison Landsberg, *Prosthetic Memory: The Transformation of American Remembrance in the Age of Mass Culture* (New York: Columbia University Press, 2004).
27 Dean Cocking and Jeroen van den Hoven, *Evil Online* (Chichester: Wiley Blackwell, 2018), 34.
28 On the temporality of the internet, see e.g. Manuel Castells, *The Rise of the Network Society* (Hoboken, NJ: John Wiley & Sons, 2011); Ben Agger, 'iTime: Labor and Life in a Smartphone Era', *Time & Society* 20, no. 1 (2011): 119–36.
29 Hubert Dreyfus, *On the Internet*, 2nd edition (New York: Routledge, 2008).
30 I've since been told by a member of Colvin's immediate family how the tweet came about. I won't spoilt it for you.

Chapter 1

1 Ruth McManus, *Death in a Digital Age* (Houndsmills: Palgrave, 2013), 45.
2 Bijan Stephen, 'Reddit Bans r/watchpeopledie in the Wake of the New Zealand Mosque Massacres', *The Verge*, 15 March 2019, https://www.theverge.com/2019/3/15/18267645/reddit-watchpeopledie-ban-new-zealand-mosque-massacre-christchurch, accessed 18 March 2019. On the

massacre and its context, see Jeff Sparrow, *Fascists among Us: Online Hate and the Christchurch Massacre* (Melbourne: Scribe, 2019).

3. Katie Mettler and Lindsey Bever, 'He Thought a Book Would Stop a Bullet. Now His Girlfriend Is Going to Jail for Killing Him', *Washington Post*, 21 December 2017, https://www.washingtonpost.com/news/morning-mix/wp/2017/12/20/he-thought-a-book-would-stop-a-bullet-now-his-girlfriend-is-going-to-jail-for-killing-him, accessed 23 April 2020.

4. Martin Gibbs, James Meese, Michael Arnold, Bjorn Nansen and Marcus Carter, '#Funeral and Instagram: Death, Social Media, and Platform Vernacular', *Information, Communication & Society* 18, no. 3 (2015): 255–68.

5. Ibid., 260.

6. Lagipoiva Cherelle Jackson, 'I Had to Stop Someone Photographing My Mother at the Morgue – Social Media Mourning Has Gone Too Far', *The Guardian*, 2 March 2020, https://www.theguardian.com/world/commentisfree/2020/mar/02/i-had-to-stop-someone-photographing-my-mother-at-the-morgue-social-media-mourning-has-gone-too-far, accessed 23 April 2020.

7. J. David Velleman, 'The Genesis of Shame', in *Self to Self: Selected Essays* (Cambridge: Cambridge University Press, 2005), 45–69.

8. Nikolaus Lehner, 'The Work of the Digital Undead: Digital Capitalism and the Suspension of Communicative Death', *Continuum: Journal of Media and Cultural Studies* 33, no. 4 (2019): 479.

9. For a further discussion of the moral problems with these 'false flag' conspiracy theories, see my 'On Some Moral Costs of Conspiracy Theory' in *Taking Conspiracy Theories Seriously*, ed. M R.X. Dentith (Lanham, MD: Rowman and Littlefield, 2018), 187–200.

10. Alexandra Topping, 'Gregg Jevin: Imaginary Comic's "Death" Tops Twitter Trends', *The Guardian*, 25 February 2012, https://www.theguardian.com/technology/2012/feb/24/gregg-jevin-death-twitter-trend, accessed 23 April 2020.

11. On the latter, see Chapter Five, 'Mixing Repertoires: Commemmoration in Digital Games and Online Worlds', in Arnold et al., *Death and Digital Media*.

12. Martin Gibbs, Marcus Carter, Michael Arnold and Bjorn Nansen, 'Serenity Now Bombs a World of Warcraft Funeral: Negotiating the Morality, Reality and Taste of Online Gaming Practices', *AoIR Selected Papers of Internet Research* 3 (2018).

13. See, for instance, Korina Giaxoglou, 'Entextualising Mourning on Facebook: Stories of Grief as Acts of Sharing', *New Review of Hypermedia and Multimedia* 21, no. 1–2 (2015): 87–105; Dorthe Refslund Christiansen,

'Death Ends a Life *Not* a Relationship: Timework and Ritualizations at Mindnet.dk', *New Review of Hypermedia and Multimedia* 21, no. 1–2 (2015): 57–71; Ishani Mukherjee and Maggie Griffith Williams, 'Death and Digi-Memorials: Perimortem and Postmortem Memory Sharing through Transitional Social Networking', *Thanatos* 3, no. 1 (2014): 160–72.

14   Margaret Gibson, 'YouTube and Bereavement Vlogging: Emotional Exchange between Strangers', *Journal of Sociology* 52, no. 4 (2016): 642.

15   The considerable literature on this topic starts from Kenneth J. Doka, *Disenfranchised Grief: Recognizing Hidden Sorrow* (Lexington, MA, England: Lexington Books, 1989).

16   'For example, site administrators have reported to us instances where the family of the deceased have been aggrieved at otherwise innocuous postings on the basis that they have been authored by people they consider complicit in the death of the deceased – for instance, an ex-lover of the deceased, the driver of a car involved in a fatal crash, and a fellow drug user in the case of an overdose'. Arnold et al., *Death and Digital Media*, 59.

17   Katie Z Gach, Casey Fiesler and Jed R. Brubaker, '"Control Your Emotions, Potter": An Analysis of Grief Policing on Facebook in Response to Celebrity Death', *Proceedings of the ACM on Human-Computer Interaction* 1, no. 47 (2017): 2. The term was coined as long ago as 1956; see Donald Horton and Richard Wohl, 'Mass Communication and Para-social Interaction: Observation on Intimacy at a Distance', *Psychiatry* 19, no. 3 (1956): 215–29.

18   Lisbeth Klastrup, '"I Didn't Know Her, but …": Parasocial Mourning of Mediated Deaths on Facebook RIP Pages', *New Review of Hypermedia and Multimedia* 21, no. 1–2 (2015): 146–64.

19   Gach et al., 'Control Your Emotions, Potter', 3.

20   Ibid., 9.

21   Arnold et al., *Death and Digital Media*, 56. On evolving norms of online mourning, see Anna J.M. Wagner, 'Do Not Click "Like" When Somebody Has Died: The Role of Norms for Mourning Practices in Social Media', *Social Media + Society* 4, no. 1 (2018): 1–11.

22   'Paul Hind Jailed After Trolling Grieving Families Online', *BBC News*, 15 November 2018, https://www.bbc.com/news/uk-england-tyne-46221066, accessed 23 April 2020.

23   Whitney Phillips, *This Is Why We Can't Have Nice Things: Mapping the Relationship between Online Trolling and Mainstream Culture* (Cambridge, MA: MIT Press, 2015), 84.

24   danah boyd, 'None of This Is Real', in *Structures of Participation in Digital Culture*, ed. Joe Karaganis (New York: Social Science Research Council, 2008), 153.

25 Karen Percy, 'Belle Gibson, Fake Wellness Blogger, Fined $410,000 Over False Cancer Claims', *ABC News*, 28 September 2017, https://www.abc.net.au/news/2017-09-28/disgraced-wellness-blogger-belle-gibson-fined/8995500, accessed 23 April 2020.

26 Howard Swains, 'The Death Bloggers', *Wired*, 17 June 2009, http://www.wired.co.uk/news/archive/2009-03/24/reports-of-my-death, accessed 23 April 2020.

27 Alina Simone, 'Death of a Troll', *The Guardian*, 28 January 2016, https://www.theguardian.com/technology/2016/jan/28/death-of-a-troll, accessed 23 April 2020. For other recent examples of faked online deaths, see Caitlin Dewey, 'The Disturbing Case of Bloggers Who Fake Death and Disease for Attention', *Washington Post*, 3 March 2015, https://www.washingtonpost.com/news/the-intersect/wp/2015/03/03/the-disturbing-case-of-the-bloggers-who-fake-death-and-disease-for-attention, accessed 23 April 2020.

28 Amelia Tate, 'Why Are Children on YouTube Saying Their Parents Are Dead?', *New Statesman*, 14 March 2017, https://www.newstatesman.com/science-tech/internet/2017/03/why-are-children-youtube-saying-their-parents-are-dead, accessed 23 April 2020.

29 Marc D. Feldman, 'Munchausen by Internet: Detecting Factitious Illness and Crisis on the Internet', *Southern Medical Journal* 93 no. 7 (2000): 669–72; *Playing Sick? Untangling the Web of Munchausen Syndrome, Munchausen by Proxy, Malingering, and Factitious Disorder* (London: Routledge, 2004).

30 Personal identity online will be a major theme in later chapters, but see also Soraj Hongladarom, 'Personal Identity and the Self in the Online and Offline World', *Minds and Machines* 21, no. 4 (2011): 533–48; Raffaele Rodogno, 'Personal Identity Online', *Philosophy and Technology* 25, no. 3 (2012): 309–28.

31 Michael Cholbi, *Grief: A Philosophical Guide* (Princeton, NJ: Princeton University Press, 2021).

32 The verb 'to catfish' came about as a result of the documentary film *Catfish* (2010), in which a journalist forms a relationship with a young woman who turns out not to exist. MTV later made a series of the same name, cementing the term. See e.g. Cocking and van den Hoven, *Evil Online*, 7–8.

33 Martin Buber, *I and Thou*, trans. Walter Kaufmann (New York: Scrivener, 1970), 77. For some discussion of Buber's understanding of encounter in relation to online communication, see Johanna Seibt and Marco Nørskov, '"Embodying" the Internet: Towards the Moral Self via Communication Robots?' *Philosophy and Technology* 25, no. 3 (2012): 285–307.

34 Timothy Burke and Jack Dickey, 'Manti Te'o's Dead Girlfriend, the Most Heartbreaking and Inspirational Story of the College Football

Season, Is a Hoax', *Deadspin*, 16 January 2013, https://deadspin.com/manti-teos-dead-girlfriend-the-most-heartbreaking-an-5976517, accessed 27 April 2020.

Chapter 2

1. Palle Yourgrau, 'The Dead', in *The Metaphysics of Death*, ed. John Martin Fischer (Stanford, CA: Stanford University Press, 1993), 140. Yourgrau has recently expanded on this metaphysics in his *Death and Nonexistence* (Oxford: Oxford University Press, 2019).
2. Lucretius, *De Rerum Natura* 3.832–42. The literature on the Lucretian Symmetry Problem is vast; start with Thomas Nagel's 'Death', in *Mortal Questions* (Cambridge: Cambridge University Press, 1979); Frederik Kaufman, 'Pre-Vital and Post-Mortem Non-Existence', *American Philosophical Quarterly* 36, no. 1 (1999): 1–19; James Warren, *Facing Death: Epicurus and His Critics* (Oxford: Oxford University Press, 2004); Mikel Burley, 'Lucretius' Symmetry Argument and the Determinacy of Death', *Philosophical Forum* 38, no. 4 (2007): 327–41; Roy Sorensen, 'The Symmetry Problem', in *The Oxford Handbook of the Philosophy of Death*, ed. Ben Bradley, Fred Feldman and Jens Johansson (Oxford: Oxford University Press. 2012), 234–53.
3. Charles Hartshorne, 'Time, Death, and Eternal Life', *The Journal of Religion* 32, no. 2 (1952): 100.
4. Yourgrau, 'The Dead', 146.
5. Hartshorne, 'Time, Death, and Eternal Life', 101. Notice that this is not an immortality in which we continue to have experienced after death. Others have suggested Hartshorne's view is compatible with such a 'subjective' immortality however; see Randall E. Auxier, 'Why One Hundred Years Is Forever: Hartshorne's Theory of Immortality', *The Personalist Forum* 14, no. 2 (1998): 109–32.
6. Marya Schechtman, 'The Story of My (Second) Life: Virtual Worlds and Narrative Identity', *Philosophy and Technology* 25, no. 3 (2012): 330.
7. Samuel Axon, 'Returning to Second Life', *Ars Technica*, 24 October 2017, https://arstechnica.com/gaming/2017/10/returning-to-second-life, accessed 24 April 2020.
8. Margaret Gibson, 'Death in *Second Life*: Lost and Missing Lives', in *Residues of Death: Disposal Refigured*, ed. Tamara Kohn, Martin Gibbs, Bjorn Nansen and Luke van Ryn (London: Routledge, 2019), 155.

9   Ibid.
10 Ibid., 156.
11 Ibid., 158, my emphasis.
12 Schechtman, 'The Story of My (Second) Life', 332.
13 Ibid., 330.
14 The classic statement of the narrative identity view is Schechtman's *The Constitution of Selves* (Ithaca, NY: Cornell University Press, 1996).
15 For my concerns with the narrative approach, see my 'Is Narrative Identity Four-Dimensionalist?', *European Journal of Philosophy* 20, no. S1 (2012): E86–E106; and 'Narrative Holism and the Moment' in *Narrative, Identity, and the Kierkegaardian Self*, ed. John Lippitt and Patrick Stokes (Edinburgh: Edinburgh University Press, 2015), 63–77.
16 It could also be operated by more than one person. That complicates the argument I'm making here but doesn't, I think, sink it.
17 Sebastian Ostritsch, 'The Amoralist Challenge to Gaming and the Gamer's Moral Obligation', *Ethics and Information Technology* 19, no. 2 (2017): 117–128; see also John McMillan and Mike King, 'Why Be Moral in a Virtual World', *Journal of Practical Ethics* 5, no. 2 (2017): 30–48.
18 On issues of adultery online see e.g. Aaron Ben-Ze'ev, *Love Online: Emotions on the Internet* (Cambridge: Cambridge University Press, 2004).
19 J. David Velleman, *Foundations for Moral Relativism* (Cambridge: Open Book Publishers, 2013), 15.
20 Bo Emerson, 'When Jimmy Carter Lusted in His Heart', *Atlanta Journal-Constitution*, 28 September 2017, https://www.ajc.com/news/when-jimmy-carter-lusted-his-heart/kzdD5pLXvT3qnf5RyJlIiK, accessed 24 April 2020.
21 Velleman, *Foundations for Moral Relativism*, 21.
22 Schechtman, 'The Story of My (Second) Life', 341.
23 Gibson, 'Death in *Second Life*', 165.
24 William Gibson, *Neuromancer* (New York: Berkley, 1989), 128.
25 Phil Agre, 'Life After Cyberspace' *EASST Review* 18, no. 2 (1999): 3–5.
26 Luciano Floridi (ed.), *The Onlife Manifesto: Being Human in a Hyperconnected Era* (Dordrecht: Springer, 2015), 1.
27 On bots, see e.g. Cocking and van den Hoven, *Evil Online*, 48.
28 David Kirkpatrick, *The Facebook Effect: The Inside Story of the Company That Is Connecting The World* (New York: Simon and Schuster, 2011), 199; cited in José van Dijck, '"You Have One Identity:" Performing the Self on Facebook and LinkedIn', *Media, Culture & Society* 35, no. 2 (2013): 199–215.
29 van Dijck, 'You Have One Identity', 201.
30 Shanyang Zhao, Sherri Grasmuck, and Jason Martin, 'Identity Construction on Facebook: Digital Empowerment in Anchored Relationships', *Computers in Human Behavior* 24 (2008): 1816–36.

31 Phillips, *This Is Why We Can't Have Nice Things*, 16.
32 Erika Pearson, 'All The World Wide Web's a Stage: The Performance of Identity in Online Social Networks', *First Monday* 14, no. 3 (2009).
33 Lauren F. Sessions, '"You Looked Better on MySpace:" Deception and Authenticity on the Web 2.0', *First Monday* 14, no. 7 (2009), drawing on Michael Hardey, 'Life beyond the Screen: Embodiment and Identity Through the Internet', *Sociological Review* 50 no. 4 (2002): 570–85.
34 On geotagging and identity-construction, see Ray Schwartz and Germaine R. Halegoua, 'The Spatial Self: Location-Based Identity Performance on Social Media', *New Media and Society* 17, no. 10 (2015): 1643–60.
35 Gretchen McCulloch, *Because Internet: Understanding How Language Is Changing* (London: Harvill Secker, 2019), 14.
36 Jake Evans, 'Mike Hall's Death Won't Be Last Time Tragedy Unfolds via Google Maps, Expert Says', *ABC News*, 9 April 2017, https://www.abc.net.au/news/2017-04-09/mike-halls-death-watched-on-google-maps-by-thousands/8415522, accessed 24 April 2020.
37 Stephanie K. Baer, 'People Are Finding Images of Their Deceased Loved Ones on Google Maps', *Buzzfeed News*, 9 January 2020, https://www.buzzfeednews.com/article/skbaer/google-maps-street-view-loved-ones-twitter, accessed 24 April 2020.
38 Margaret Gibson and Clarissa Carden, *Living and Dying in a Virtual World: Digital Kinships, Nostalgia, and Mourning in Second Life* (Houndsmills: Palgrave, 2018), 3.
39 Cocking and van den Hoven, *Evil Online*, 50.
40 boyd, 'None of This Is Real'.
41 Again, there's a vast literature here, but good places to start include Charles Guignon, *On Being Authentic* (London: Routledge, 2004), and Somogy Varga, *Authenticity as an Ethical Ideal* (London: Routledge, 2012).
42 Harry Frankfurt, 'On Bullshit', in *The Importance of What We Care About: Philosophical Essays* (Cambridge: Cambridge University Press, 1988), 117–33.
43 Schechtman, *The Constitution of Selves*, 119–30; see also John Lippitt, 'Getting the Story Straight: Kierkegaard, MacIntyre, and Some Problems with Narrative', *Inquiry* 50, no. 1 (2007): 34–69.
44 Erving Goffman, *The Presentation of Self in Everyday Life* (New York: Anchor Books, 1959).
45 Sessions, 'You Looked Better on MySpace'.
46 Zhao, Grasmuck, and Martin, 'Identity Construction on Facebook', 1828.
47 Stanley Cavell, *Cities of Words: Pedagogical Letters on a Register of the Moral Life* (Cambridge, MA: Harvard University Press, 2005).
48 van Dijck, 'You Have One Identity', 203.

49 boyd, 'None of This Is Real'; Joanne Garde-Hanson, 'My Memories? Personal Digital Archive Fever and Facebook', in *Save As ...: Digital Memories*, ed. Joanne Garde-Hansen, Andrew Hoskins and Anna Reader (Houndsmills: Palgrave, 2009), 135–50.
50 Zhao, Grasmuck, and Martin, 'Identity Construction on Facebook'.
51 On the effects of format on online grieving, see Pamela Roberts, '2 People Like This: Mourning According to Format', *Bereavement Care* 31, no. 2 (2012): 55–61.
52 Hilde Lindemann discusses the ways in which pregnant women 'call into personhood' the foetus they are carrying through activities such as setting up a nursery, giving it a nickname, and so on. Karthyn Norlock raises this as a possible counter-example to her claim that we have real relationships to the dead, but ultimately finds partial support in it instead: our relationship to foetuses, like our relationship to the dead, is one where real and imaginal elements overlap. Marya Schechtman, who draws on Lindemann's account of how third-personal ascriptions can constitute persons, also discusses the ways in which we go on to treat infants as socially situated. Hilde Lindemann, 'Miscarriage and the Stories we Live By', *Journal of Social Philosophy* 46, no. 1 (2015): 80–90; Norlock, 'Real (and) Imaginal Relationships with the Dead', 353; Marya Schechtman, *Staying Alive: Personal Identity, Practical Concerns, and the Unity of a Life* (Oxford: Oxford University Press, 2014), 104–5.
53 Alasdair MacIntyre, *After Virtue* (Notre Dame, IN: University of Notre Dame Press, 1984), 99.

Chapter 3

1 Søren Kierkegaard, *Søren Kierkegaard's Journals and Papers*, vol. 2, ed. and trans. Howard V. Hong and Edna H. Hong (Bloomington, IN: Indiana University Press, 1970), 482–3.
2 For more, see Patrick Stokes, 'Kierkegaard's Critique of the Internet', in *Kierkegaard and Issues in Contemporary Ethics*, ed. Mélissa Fox-Muraton (Berlin: Walter de Gruyter, 2020), 125–45.
3 Arnold et al., *Death and Digital Media*, 118.
4 Jeremy Grange, 'Resusci Anne and L'Inconnue: The Mona Lisa of the Seine', *BBC News*, 16 October 2013, https://www.bbc.com/news/magazine-24534069, accessed 24 April 2020.
5 Margaret Gibson, *Objects of the Dead: Mourning and Memory in Everyday Life* (Melbourne: Melbourne University Press, 2008), 81.

6   Walter Benjamin, *Illuminations*, trans. Harry Zohn (London: Fontana, 1992), 214.
7   Ibid., 219.
8   Roland Barthes, *Camera Lucida: Reflections on Photography*, trans. Richard Howard (London: Vintage, 2000), 96. Cora Diamond notes a similar phenomenon in her discussion of Ted Hughes' poem 'Six Young Men', which plays on the ambiguous life in a 1914 photo of six men who had all died six months after the photo was taken. Cora Diamond, 'The Difficulty of Reality and the Difficulty of Philosophy', *Partial Answers: Journal of Literature and the History of Ideas* 1, no. 2 (2003): 1–26. Thanks to Christopher Cordner for pointing me towards this.
9   Barthes, *Camera Lucida*, 87–8.
10 E.M. Forster, *The Eternal Moment and Other Stories* (San Diego: Harcourt Brace Jovanovich, 1956), 4.
11 Dreyfus, *On the Internet*, 49–50, 68–71.
12 Arnold et al., *Death and Digital Media*, 113. As I write this, Australia has restricted funerals to a maximum of ten attendees to prevent the spread of COVID-19; the funeral industry is now trying to work out how to use telepresence technology more effectively.
13 For an excellent overview, see Matthew Lombard and Matthew T. Jones 'Defining Presence', in *Immersed in Media: Telepresence Theory, Measurement, and Technology*, ed. Matthew Lombard, Frank Biocca, Jonathan Freeman, Wijnand IJsselsteijn and Rachel J. Schaevitz (Dordrecht: Springer, 2015), 13–34.
14 Goffman, *The Presentation of Self in Everyday Life*, 17. See also Kathleen M. Cumiskey and Larissa Hjorth *Haunting Hands: Mobile Media Practices and Loss* (Oxford: Oxford University Press, 2017), 26–7.
15 The term 'telepresence' was first popularized in 1980 by Marvin Minsky, whose discussion was about manipulating objects remotely with the feeling as if one were located with those objects; for instance, operating a robot arm to clean up the remains of a nuclear meltdown. Marvin Minsky, 'Telepresence', *OMNI Magazine* 2, 45–52.
16 Dreyfus, 'On the Internet', 69.
17 For a strong rebuttal to Dreyfus' claims about the necessary links between trust, vulnerability, and presence, see Thomas W. Simpson 'Telepresence and Trust: A Speech-Act Theory of Mediated Communication', *Philosophy and Technology* 30, no. 4 (2017): 443–59.
18 Shannon Sims, 'The End of American Prison Visits: Jails End Face-to-Face Contact – And Families Suffer', *The Guardian*, 10 December 2017, https://www.theguardian.com/us-news/2017/dec/09/skype-for-jailed-video-calls-prisons-replace-in-person-visits, accessed 24 April 2020.

19 Luciano Floridi, *The Ethics of Information* (Oxford: Oxford University Press, 2013), 37–9.
20 Maurice Merleau-Ponty, *Phenomenology of Perception*, trans. Donald A. Landes (London: Routledge, 2011), 144.
21 Don Ihde, *Bodies in Technology* (Minneapolis: University of Minnesota Press, 2002), 14.
22 Ihde, *Bodies in Technology*, 8.
23 Richard L. Daft and Robert H. Lengel, 'Organizational Information Requirements, Media Richness and Structural Design', *Management Science* 32, no. 5 (1986): 513–644.
24 Simpson, 'Telepresence and Trust'.
25 Or if we're four-dimensionalists about persons: where a specific person-stage is at a given time.
26 Richard Heersmink, 'Distributed Selves: Personal Identity and Extended Memory Systems', *Synthese* 194, no. 8 (2017): 3149.
27 Andy Clark, 'Re-Inventing Ourselves: The Plasticity of Embodiment, Sensing, and Mind', *Journal of Medicine and Philosophy* 32, no. 3 (2007): 278.
28 Landsberg, *Prosthetic Memory*.
29 McManus, *Death in a Global Age*, 141.

Chapter 4

1 Italo Calvino, *Invisible Cities*, trans. William Weaver (San Diego: Harcourt Brace, 1974), 109.
2 Ibid., 110.
3 This is just one of the things that makes dying as a process so conceptually complex; see e.g. Fred Feldman, *Confrontations with the Reaper: A Philosophical Study of the Nature and Value of Death* (Oxford: Oxford University Press, 1992), 72–88.
4 There is a sizeable literature on the difficulties of defining death; I'd suggest starting with Christopher Belshaw, *Annihilation: The Sense and Significance of Death* (Montreal: McGill-Queen's University Press, 2009); Steven Luper, *The Philosophy of Death* (Cambridge: Cambridge University Press, 2012); Cody Gilmore, 'When Do Things Die?' in *The Oxford Handbook of the Philosophy of Death*, ed. Ben Bradley, Fred Feldman, and Jens Johansson (Oxford: Oxford University Press, 2013), 5–59.
5 Dimitri Tsintjilonis, 'Death and the Sacrifice of Signs: "Measuring" the Dead in Tana Toraja', *Oceania* 71, no.1 (2000): 5.

6   For some vivid depictions of Torajan death practices and particularly ma'nene, see Jewel Topsfield, and Amilia Rosa, 'Life Among the Dead', *Sydney Morning Herald*, 29 August 2017, https://www.smh.com.au/interactive/2017/toraja-death-ritual, accessed 24 April 2020; Claudio Sieber, 'Cleaning the Dead: The Afterlife Rituals of the Torajan People', *The Guardian*, 13 October 2017, https://www.theguardian.com/world/gallery/2017/oct/13/cleaning-the-dead-the-afterlife-rituals-of-the-torajan-people, accessed 24 April 2020.
7   Ludwig Wittgenstein, *Zettel*, ed. G.E.M. Anscombe and G.H. von Wright, trans. G.E.M. Anscombe (Berkeley: University of California Press, 1967), 40.
8   Name changed.
9   Jaweed Kaleem, 'Death on Facebook Now Common as "Dead Profiles" Create Vast Virtual Cemetery', *Huffington Post*, 12 July 2012, http://www.huffingtonpost.com/2012/12/07/death-facebook-dead-profiles_n_2245397.html, accessed 24 April 2020.
10 Carl J. Öhman and David Watson, 'Are the Dead Taking Over Facebook? A Big Data Approach to the Future of Death Online', *Big Data & Society* 6, no. 1 (2019): 1–13.
11 Carl Öhman and Luciano Floridi, 'The Political Economy of Death in the Age of Information: A Critical Approach to the Digital Afterlife Industry', *Mind and Machines* 27, no. 4 (2017): 639–62. See also Tero Karppi, 'Death Proof: On the Biopolitics and Noopolitics of Memorializing Dead Facebook Users', *Culture Machine* 14 (2017): 1–20.
12 Alex Lambert, Bjorn Nansen, and Michael Arnold, 'Algorithmic Memorial Videos: Contextualising Automated Curation', *Memory Studies* 11, no. 2 (2018): 156–71. On some of the distressing and unwelcome ways the dead reappear on social media, see Selina Ellis Gray, 'The Memory Remains: Visible Presences within the Network', *Thanatos* 3, no. 1 (2014): 127–40.
13 Max Kelly, 'Memories of Friends Departed Endure on Facebook', *The Facebook Blog*, 26 October 2009, https://www.facebook.com/notes/facebook-app/memories-of-friends-departed-endure-on-facebook/163091042130, accessed 24 April 2020.
14 Pamela Roberts, 'The Living and the Dead: Community in the Virtual Cemetery', *Omega: Journal of Death & Dying* 49, no. 1 (2004): 57–76; Tony Walter, Rachid Hourizi, Wendy Moncur and Stacey Pitsillides, 'Does the Internet Change How We Die and Mourn? Overview and Analysis', *Omega: Journal of Death & Dying* 64, no. 4 (2011): 275–302; Jed R. Brubaker and Gillian Hayes, '"We Will Never Forget You [online]": An Empirical Investigation of Post-Mortem Myspace Comments', Proceedings of the ACM 2011 Conference on Computer Supported Cooperative Work,

123–32; Amanda L. Williams and Michael J. Merten, 'Adolescents' Online Social Networking Following the Death of a Peer', *Journal of Adolescent Research* 24, no. 1 (2009): 67–90; Elaine Kasket, 'Being-towards-death in the Digital Age', *Existential Analysis: Journal of the Society for Existential Analysis* 23, no. 2 (2012): 249–61; Rebecca Kern, Abbe E. Forman and Gisela Gil-Egui, 'R.I.P.: Remain in Perpetuity. Facebook Memorial Pages', *Telematics and Informatics* 30, no. 1 (2013): 2–10; Jed R. Brubaker, Gillian Hayes and Paul Dourish, 'Beyond the Grave: Facebook as a Site for the Expansion of Death and Mourning', *The Information Society* 29, no. 3 (2013): 152–63; Erin Willis and Patrick Ferrucci, 'Mourning and Grief on Facebook: An Examination of Motives for Interacting with the Deceased' *Omega* 76, no. 2 (2017): 122–40; Molly Kalan, 'Expressions of Grief on Facebook: The Complicated Nature of Online Memorialization for the Bereaved', *Interface* 1, no. 1 (2014): 1–15; Jessica Blower and Rachael Sharman, 'To Grieve or Not to Grieve (Online)? Interactions with Deceased Facebook Friends', *Death Studies* (2019, online early).

15 Robert Dobler, 'Ghosts in the Machine: Mourning the MySpace Dead', in *Folklore and the Internet: Vernacular Expression in a Digital World*, ed. Trevor Blank (Logan, UT: Utah State University Press, 2009), 175–93.

16 Kasket, *All the Ghosts in the Machine*, 54.

17 For a number of these cases, see Cumiskey and Hjorth, *Haunting Hands*, 163–73.

18 Sarah Young, 'Woman Who Texted Late Father's Phone for Four Years Receives Heartwarming Reply from New Owner', *The Independent*, 28 October 2019, https://www.independent.co.uk/life-style/woman-text-message-dead-father-response-phone-a9174151.html, accessed 24 April 2020. The sequel to this story is not quite so heartening; I'll leave it up to you whether you want to seek it out or not.

19 Kern et al., 'R.I.P.: Remain in Perpetuity', 66; Kasket, 'Being-towards-death in the Digital Age'; Erinn Staley, 'Messaging the Dead: Social Network Sites and Theologies of Afterlife', in *Digital Death: Mortality and Beyond in an Online Age*, ed. Christopher M. Moreman and A. David Lewis (Santa Barbara, CA: Praeger, 2014), 9–21.

20 Kasket, *All the Ghosts in the Machine*, 54.

21 Cumiskey and Hjorth, *Haunting Hands*, 163–73.

22 K. Mitch Hodge, 'On Imagining the Afterlife', *Journal of Cognition and Culture* 11, no. 2 (2011): 376–89.

23 Kasket, 'Being-Towards-Death in the Digital Age.'

24 Neil McMahon, 'The Last Word: Profiles Live On After Death', *Sydney Morning Herald*, 28 May 2011, https://www.smh.com.au/technology/the-

last-word-profiles-live-on-after-death-20110528-1f9bo.html, accessed 24 April 2020.
25 Arnold et al., *Death and Digital Media*, 54.
26 Gibson and Carden, *Living and Dying in a Virtual World*.
27 E.g. Jessa Lingel, 'The Digital Remains: Social Media and Practices of Online Grief' *The Information Society* 29, no. 3 (2013): 190–5; Nicola Wright, 'Death and the Internet: The Implications of the Digital Afterlife', *First Monday* 19, no. 6 (2014); Margaret Gibson, 'Digital Objects of the Dead: Negotiating Electronic Remains', in *The Social Construction of Death: Interdisciplinary Perspectives*, ed. Leen Van Brussel and Nico Carpentier (Houndsmills: Palgrave, 2014), 221–38.
28 Feldman, *Confrontations with the Reaper*, 89–105. Among those who do not accept it, in addition to Feldman and David Mackie, are Palle Yourgrau and Niall Connolly, appealing to the being of nonexistent objects. See Yourgrau, 'The Dead'; Niall Connolly, 'How the Dead Live', *Philosophia* 39, no. 1 (2011): 83–103.
29 Belshaw, *Annihilation*, 129.
30 Aristotle, *Eudemian Ethics*, 1235a,b.
31 Robert Pogue Harrison, *The Dominion of the Dead* (Chicago: University of Chicago Press, 2003), 147.
32 Ibid., 92.
33 Raimond Gaita, *The Philosopher's Dog* (Melbourne: Text Publishing, 2002), 94.
34 Yourgrau, 'The Dead', 138.
35 Aristotle, *Nichomachean Ethics*, 1101a.
36 Again, the literature is intimidatingly big, but start with Nagel, *Mortal Questions*; Fischer (ed.), *The Metaphysics of Death*; Ben Bradley, *Well-Being and Death* (Oxford: Oxford University Press, 2003); Belshaw, *Annihilation*.
37 Henrik Ibsen, *Vildanden*, http://www.gutenberg.org/cache/epub/13041/pg13041-images.html, accessed 24 April 2020, my translation.
38 Bernie Hogan and Anabel Quan-Haase, 'Persistence and Change in Social Media', *Bulletin of Science, Technology & Society* 30, no. 5 (2010): 312.
39 Harrison, *The Dominion of the Dead*, 147–8.
40 Ibid., 148.
41 For the claim that persons survive as dead bodies, in a radically degraded way, see e.g. David Mackie, 'Personal Identity and Dead People', *Philosophical Studies* 95, no. 3 (1999): 219–42; Patrick Stokes, 'Are There Dead Persons?', *Canadian Journal of Philosophy* 49, no. 6 (2019): 755–75.
42 Apart from unease about quoting Woody Allen at all, the quote's provenance is unclear; as Adam Buben notes, 'This oft-quoted passage is

usually attributed to *The Illustrated Woody Allen Reader*, or to *On Being Funny*. Oddly, these books only include the first sentence of the passage, while there is no clear source for the second sentence.' Adam Buben, 'Technology of the Dead: Objects of Loving Remembrance or Replaceable Resources?', *Philosophical Papers* 44, no. 1 (2015): 15 n.1.

43 Kathy Behrendt, 'A Special Way of Being Afraid', *Philosophical Psychology* 23, no. 5 (2010): 669–82.

44 David Lewis, 'Survival and Identity', in *Philosophical Papers*, vol. 1 (Oxford: Oxford University Press, 1983), 17.

45 Mark Johnston, *Surviving Death* (Princeton, NJ: Princeton University Press, 2010), 175.

46 Tom Stoppard, *Rosencrantz and Guildenstern Are Dead* (London: Faber, 1967), 52.

47 Buben helpfully casts the history of the philosophy of death as a struggle between two contrasting views, which we can broadly call 'Platonic' and 'Epicurean.' He argues that in Kierkegaard and Heidegger a new, third approach appears. Adam Buben, *Meaning and Mortality in Kierkegaard and Heidegger: Origins of the Existential Philosophy of Death* (Evanston, IL: Northwestern University Press, 2016).

48 See e.g. Patrick Stokes, *The Naked Self: Kierkegaard and Personal Identity* (Oxford: Oxford University Press, 2015); 'Temporal Asymmetry and the Self/Person Split' *Journal of Value Inquiry* 51, no.2 (2017): 203–19.

49 Schechtman, *Staying Alive*.

50 For a phenomenological account of the ways in which presence and absence relate to each other in the experience of grief, see Matthew Ratcliffe, 'Relating to the Dead: Social Cognition and the Phenomenology of Grief', in *Phenomenology of Sociality: Discovering the 'We'*, ed. Thomas Szanto and Dermot Moran (London: Routledge, 2015), 202–15.

51 Kevin O'Neill *Internet Afterlife: Virtual Salvation in the 21st Century* (Santa Barbara: Praeger, 2016).

52 Poul Ricoeur, *Oneself as Another* trans. Kathleen Blamey (Chicago: University of Chicago Press, 1992), 160.

53 The Bob Hope example was raised in discussion during a postgraduate seminar at the University of Melbourne in 2003; regrettably I cannot now recall who suggested it.

54 For an overview of how some of the medical, ethical, and policy issues around defining death hang together, see Robert H. Blank, 'Technology and Death Policy: Redefining Death', *Mortality* 6, no. 2 (2001): 191–202.

55 Antonia Farzan, 'An Inmate Claims His Life Sentence Ended When He Died and Was Revived. Nice Try, Court Rules', *The Washington Post*, 8 November 2019, https://www.washingtonpost.com/nation/2019/11/08/

benjamin-schreiber-denied-life-sentence-appeal-iowa, accessed 24 April 2020.
56 See e.g. Feldman, *Confrontations with the Reaper*, 62–6. For the record: it's a myth that Walt Disney is in cryonic suspension. He was cremated.

Chapter 5

1 'Mind the Gap Tube Announcement Returns after Wife's Plea', *BBC News*, 9 March 2013, https://www.bbc.com/news/uk-england-london-21719848, accessed 24 April 2020; Claire Burke, 'The Christmas Story of One Tube Station's "Mind the Gap" Voice', *The Guardian*, 25 December 2019, https://www.theguardian.com/cities/2019/dec/25/the-christmas-story-of-one-tube-stations-mind-the-gap-voice, accessed 24 April 2020.
2 City of Melbourne, 'Old Melbourne Cemetery', https://www.melbourne.vic.gov.au/building-and-development/urban-planning/local-area-planning/queen-victoria-market-precinct-renewal-plan/history-heritage/Pages/old-melbourne-cemetery.aspx, accessed 4 April 2020.
3 As best I can tell, this is a *very* rough paraphrase of 'we may fancy the life after death to be as a second life, into which a man enters in the figure, or the picture, or the inscription, and lives longer there than when he was really alive. Bur this figure also, this second existence, dies out too, sooner or later. Time will not allow himself to be cheated of his rights with the monuments of men or with themselves'. Johann Wolfgang von Goethe, *Elective Affinities* (New York: Henry Holt, 1872), 166.
4 Iain Mackenzie, 'Domesday Project Reborn Online after 25 Years', *BBC News*, 12 May 2011, https://www.bbc.com/news/technology-13367398, accessed 24 April 2020.
5 Viktor Mayer-Schönberger, *Delete: The Virtue of Forgetting in the Digital Age* (Princeton, NJ: Princeton University Press, 2009), 68.
6 Kasket, *All the Ghosts in the Machine*, 183.
7 https://onlineafterdeath.weebly.com, accessed 9 April 2020.
8 Heidi Ebert, 'Profiles of the Dead: Mourning and Memorial on Facebook', in *Digital Death: Mortality and Beyond in an Online Age*, ed. Christopher M. Moreman and A. David Lewis (Santa Barbara: Praeger, 2014), 23–42.
9 The nature (and limits) of Lewis' grief are treated at length in Michael Cholbi's forthcoming *Grief: A Philosophical Guide*.
10 C.S. Lewis, *A Grief Observed* (London: Faber, 1961), 18.
11 Öhman and Watson, 'Are the Dead Taking Over Facebook?', 2.

12 Ibid., 10.
13 Epicurus, 'Letter to Menoeceus', Diogenes Laertius 10.124.
14 Søren Kierkegaard, *Three Discourses on Imagined Occasions*, ed. and trans. Howard V. Hong and Edna H. Hong (Princeton, NJ: Princeton University Press, 1993), 74.
15 Søren Kierkegaard, 'The Work of Love in Recollecting One Who Is Dead', in *Works of Love*, ed. and trans. Howard V. Hong and Edna H. Hong (Princeton, NJ: Princeton University Press, 1995), 345–58.
16 For some objections to these arguments, see e.g. Belshaw, *Annihilation*; Stephen Winter, 'Against Posthumous Rights', *Journal of Applied Philosophy* 27, no. 2 (2010): 186–99; James Stacey Taylor, *Death, Posthumous Harms, and Bioethics* (London: Routledge, 2012).
17 Jeffrey Blustein *The Moral Demands of Memory* (Cambridge: Cambridge University Press, 2008), 277–8.
18 Janna Thompson, 'Inherited Obligations and Generational Continuity', *Canadian Journal of Philosophy* 29, no. 4 (1999): 493–515.
19 Michelle Stacey, 'Writ on Water', *The Paris Review*, 23 February 2016, https://www.theparisreview.org/blog/2016/02/23/writ-in-water, accessed 24 April 2020.
20 Blustein, *The Moral Demands of Memory*, 275.
21 Aristotle, *Eudemian Ethics* 1239b.
22 Taylor, *Death, Posthumous Harms, and Bioethics*, 59.
23 Thanks to Jason Brown for help with getting this formulation right.
24 Gaita, *The Philosopher's Dog*, 89.
25 'Jimmy Savile's Headstone Removed from Scarborough Cemetery', *BBC News*, 10 October 2012, https://www.bbc.com/news/uk-england-york-north-yorkshire-19893373, accessed 24 April 2020.
26 Sparrow, *Fascists Among Us*, 2.
27 It's also possible to conclude, as Christopher Belshaw notes, that even if there are posthumous harms, they are of 'vanishingly low importance'. Belshaw himself does not accept that there are posthumous harms, but does allow for possible instrumental benefit in respecting the wishes of the dead. Belshaw, *Annihilation*, 151.
28 John Harris, 'Doing Posthumous Harm', in *The Metaphysics and Ethics of Death: New Essays*, ed. James Stacey Taylor (Oxford: Oxford University Press, 2013), 215.
29 Edina Harbinja has done important work on this topic from a legal perspective in recent years; see e.g 'Post-mortem Privacy 2.0: Theory, Law, and Technology', *International Review of Law, Computers & Technology* 31, no. 1 (2017): 26–42; 'The Inheritance of Digital Media', in *Partners for*

Preservation: Advancing Digital Preservation Through Cross-Community Collaboration, ed. Jeanne Kramer-Smyth (London: Facet, 2018), 3–24.
30 On why these are such an unusual class of assets, see Natalie M. Banta, 'Inherit the Cloud: The Role of Private Contracts in Distributing or Deleting Digital Assets at Death', *Fordham Law Review* 83, no. 2 (2014): 799–854.
31 Jed R. Brubaker, Lynn Dombrowski, Anita M. Gilbert, Nafiri Kusumakaulika, and Gillian R. Hayes, 'Stewarding a Legacy: Responsibilities and Relationships in the Management of Post-mortem Data', Association for Computing Machinery Conference on Human Factors in Computing Systems (CHI), Toronto, 2014, https://cmci.colorado.edu/idlab/assets/bibliography/pdf/Brubaker2014a.pdf, accessed 13 April 2020.
32 Kasket, *All The Ghosts in the Machine*, 38.
33 'Facebook: Court Rules Parents Have Rights to Dead Daughter's Account', *Deutche Welle*, 12 July 2018, https://www.dw.com/en/facebook-court-rules-parents-have-rights-to-dead-daughters-account/a-44642230, accessed 24 April 2020.
34 'Berlin Court Rules Grieving Parents Have No Right to Dead Child's Facebook Account', *Deutche Welle*, 31 May 2017, https://www.dw.com/en/berlin-court-rules-grieving-parents-have-no-right-to-dead-childs-facebook-account/a-39064843, accessed 24 April 2020.
35 I provide a more technical working-out of some of these considerations in 'The Decay of Digital Personhood: Towards New Norms of Disposal and Preservation', in *Residues of Death*, ed. Kohn, Gibbs Nansen and van Ryn (London: Routledge, 2019), 80–90.
36 Jacques Derrida, *Archive Fever: A Freudian Impression*, trans. Eric Prenowitz (Chicago and London: University of Chicago Press, 1996), 3.
37 Luciano Floridi, *The Fourth Revolution: How the Infosphere Is Reshaping Human Reality* (Oxford: Oxford University Press, 2014), 125.
38 Harrison, *The Dominion of the Dead*, 153.

Chapter 6

1 The fullest account of Roman Mazurenko's story is Casey Newton's 'Speak, Memory', *The Verge*, 6 October 2016, https://www.theverge.com/a/luka-artificial-intelligence-memorial-roman-mazurenko-bot, accessed 24 April 2020.

2   Tama Leaver, 'Posthumous Performance and Digital Resurrection: From Science Fiction to Start-Ups', in *Residues of Death*, ed. Kohn, Gibbs Nansen and van Ryn, 78.
3   Officially its name was 'Clippit', but 'Clippy' seems to have stuck.
4   For a discussion of chatbots of the dead and the uncanny valley, see Debra J. Bassett, 'Ctrl+Alt+Delete: The Changing Landscape of the Uncanny Valley and the Fear of Second Loss', *Current Psychology* (2018, online early), https://doi.org/10.1007/s12144-018-0006-5.
5   Kashmir Hill, 'This Startup Promised 10,000 People Eternal Digital Life – Then It Died', *Splinter*, 9 April 2015, https://splinternews.com/this-start-up-promised-10-000-people-eternal-digital-li-1793847011, accessed 24 April 2020.
6   Will Coldwell, 'Why Death Is Not The End of Your Social Media Life', *The Guardian*, 18 February 2013, https://www.theguardian.com/media/shortcuts/2013/feb/18/death-social-media-liveson-deadsocial, accessed 24 April 2020.
7   Isobel Asher Hamilton, 'These 2 Tech Founders Lost Their Friends in Tragic Accidents. Now They Have Built AI Chatbots to Give People Life after Death', *Business Insider Australia*, 16 November 2018, https://www.businessinsider.com.au/eternime-and-replika-giving-life-to-the-dead-with-new-technology-2018-11, accessed 24 April 2020.
8   Laura Parker, 'How to Become Virtually Immortal', *The New Yorker*, 4 April 2014, https://www.newyorker.com/tech/annals-of-technology/how-to-become-virtually-immortal, accessed 24 April 2020.
9   Leaver, 'Posthumous Performance and Digital Resurrection', 72.
10 Michelle Starr, 'EterniMe Wants You to Live Forever as a Digital Ghost', *CNet*, 21 April 2017, https://www.cnet.com/news/eternime-wants-you-to-live-forever-as-a-digital-ghost, accessed 24 April 2020.
11 https://www.eter9.com, accessed 25 February 2020.
12 Buben, 'Technology of the Dead', 19.
13 Alex Ritman, 'James Dean Reborn in CGI For Vietnam War Action-Drama', *Hollywood Reporter*, 6 November 2019, https://www.hollywoodreporter.com/news/afm-james-dean-reborn-cgi-vietnam-war-action-drama-1252703, accessed 24 April 2020.
14 https://basehologram.com, accessed 6 April 2020; for an interestingly deflationary review of the experience, see Will Gompertz, 'Whitney Houston: Will Gompertz Reviews Hologram Show in Sheffield', *BBC News*, 29 February 2020, https://www.bbc.com/news/entertainment-arts-51636482, accessed 24 April 2020.
15 'Virtual Reality Reunites Mother with Dead Daughter, Bringing Tears but also Helping Her Let Go of Child She Has Missed So Dearly', *South China*

Morning Post, 12 February 2020, https://www.scmp.com/lifestyle/family-relationships/article/3049985/mother-cries-when-reuniting-dead-daughter-vr-learns, accessed 24 April 2020.

16 Predictably, this technology has been used primarily to produce porn videos featuring women who never consented for their face to be used in this way. On the ethical challenges of deepfakes, see Carl Öhman, 'Introducing the Pervert's Dilemma: A Contribution to the Critique of Deepfake Pornography', *Ethics and Information Technology* 22, no. 2 (2020): 133–40.

17 'South Korean Mother "Reunites" with Dead Daughter Using Virtual Reality Technology', *SBS News*, 15 February 2020, https://www.sbs.com.au/news/south-korean-mother-reunites-with-dead-daughter-using-virtual-reality-technology, accessed 24 April 2020.

18 Thomas Nagel, 'What Is It Like to Be a Bat?', in *Mortal Questions*, 165–80.

19 Arielle Pardes, 'The Emotional Chatbots Are Here to Probe Our Feelings', *Wired*, 31 January 2018, https://www.wired.com/story/replika-open-source, accessed 24 April 2020.

20 Olivia Solon, 'Joey from Friends Becomes First Tv Star to Be "Virtually Immortalized"', *The Guardian*, 16 October 2016, https://www.theguardian.com/technology/2016/oct/20/joey-friends-virtual-digital-avatar-chatbot, accessed 24 April 2020.

21 Andrew Griffin, 'App Lets People Easily Take Photos with any Dead Person They Like and Bring Them "Back To Life"', *The Independent*, 3 March 2017, https://www.independent.co.uk/life-style/gadgets-and-tech/news/elrois-app-selfie-dead-friends-family-celebrity-3d-scan-mwc-mobile-world-congress-a7610331.html, accessed 24 April 2020.

22 John Locke, *An Essay Concerning Human Understanding*, ed. Peter H. Nidditch (Oxford: Clarendon Press, 1975), 341–2.

23 Derek Parfit, *Reasons and Persons* (Oxford: Oxford University Press, 1984), 199–01.

24 Robert Nozick, *Philosophical Explanations* (Cambridge, MA: Harvard University Press, 1981), 29–43.

25 Raymond Martin, *Self-Concern: An Experiential Approach to What Matters in Survival* (Cambridge: Cambridge University Press, 1998).

26 See e.g. Parfit, *Reasons and Persons*, 327; Marya Schechtman, 'Empathic Access: The Missing Ingredient in Personal Identity', in *Personal Identity*, ed. Raymond Martin and John Barresi (Maldon, MA: Blackwell, 2003), 238–59; Simon Beck, 'Going Narrative: Schechtman and the Russians', *South African Journal of Philosophy* 27, no. 2 (2008): 69–79.; Stokes, *The Naked Self*, 121–4.

27 Arnold et al., *Death and Digital Media*, 135–6.

28 Almereyda Michael, *Marjorie Prime* [film], Dir. Michael Almereyda (USA: BB Film, 2017).
29 George Harrison, 'In Lovemaking Memory: Sex Robots Are Being Made to Look Like Customers' Dead Wives… And One Firm Insists It's the Best Way to Help with Their Grief', *The Sun*, 14 August 2017, https://www.thesun.co.uk/living/4230725/sex-robots-dead-wives-customisation, accessed 24 April 2020.
30 Though as Barthes notes, a photograph, by imposing itself on us, can actually displace memory rather than enhancing it. Barthes, *Camera Lucida*, 91.
31 Jacques Derrida, *The Work of Mourning* (Chicago: University of Chicago Press, 2001), 38.
32 Buben, 'Technology of the Dead', 26 n. 16.
33 Ibid., 20–1.
34 Ibid., 25, my emphasis.
35 Alexis Elder, 'Conversation from Beyond the Grave? A Neo-Confucian Ethics of Chatbots of the Dead', *Journal of Applied Philosophy* 37, no. 1 (2020): 76.
36 Martin Heidegger, 'The Question Concerning Technology', in *Basic Writings*, ed. and trans. David Farrel Krell (New York: HarperCollins, 1993).
37 Derrida, *The Work of Mourning*, 224 n. 3.
38 Buben, 'Technology of the Dead', 28.
39 Martha Nussbaum has argued that treating people as fungible is one of the ways in which we objectify others, including sexually. See her 'Objectification', *Philosophy and Public Affairs* 24, no. 4 (1995): 249–91.
40 Lewis, *A Grief Observed*, 18–19.
41 Ibid., 44.
42 Elder, 'Conversation from Beyond the Grave?'

Chapter 7

1 Charlie Brooker, 'Be Right Back', *Black Mirror* [TV program] Dir. Owen Harris (UK: Zeppotron, 2013).
2 Leaver, 'Posthumous Performance and Digital Resurrection', 71.
3 Derrida, *The Work of Mourning*, 159.
4 Ibid., 160.
5 Jacques Derrida, *Memoires for Paul de Man*, trans. Cecile Lindsay (New York: Columbia University Press, 1989), 21.

6 Lewis, *A Grief Observed*, 17.
7 Ibid., 18.
8 Ibid., 9.
9 Kathryn J. Norlock discusses this experience in her excellent 'Real (and) Imaginal Relationships with the Dead'.
10 Derrida, *The Work of Mourning*, 89.
11 Jean-Paul Sartre, *The Psychology of Imagination* (London: Methuen, 1972), 8. On this, see, Christopher Jude McCarroll and John Sutton, 'Multiperspectival Imagery: Sartre and Cognitive Theory on Point of View in Remembering and Imagining', in *Phenomenology and Science: Confrontations and Convergence*, ed. Jack Reynolds and Richard Sebold (Houndsmills: Palgrave, 2016), 181–204.
12 Lewis, *A Grief Observed*, 19.
13 Emmanuel Levinas, *Totality and Infinity: An Essay on Exteriority*, trans. Alfonso Lingis (Pittsburgh: Duquesne University Press, 1969).
14 Jean-Paul Sartre, *Being and Nothingness*, trans. Hazel E. Barnes (London: Routledge, 1969), 254–5.
15 Derrida, *The Work of Mourning*, 161.
16 Ibid., 206.
17 Ibid., 115.
18 Ibid., 116.
19 Lewis, *A Grief Observed*, 56.
20 Derrida, *The Work of Mourning*, 47.
21 One could imagine the Ash avatar, being privy to all of Ash's online communication, telling Martha something about Ash she didn't know; that might count as an instance of the dead surprising the living, but in a far more indirect way than is usually the case with human spontaneity. The 'new' fact was already in the world, and Martha could (in theory) have learned it some other way.
22 Gabe Cohen, 'AI Art at Christies Sells for $432,500', *New York Times*, 25 October 2018, https://www.nytimes.com/2018/10/25/arts/design/ai-art-sold-christies.html, accessed 24 April 2020.
23 Lehner, 'The Work of the Digital Undead', 481.
24 Ibid., 482.
25 Ihde, *Bodies in Technology*, 104–5.
26 Elder, 'Conversations from Beyond the Grave?', 86.
27 Ibid., 76.
28 Martin Heidegger, *Being and Time*, trans. Joan Stambaugh (Albany, NY: SUNY Press, 2010), 68–70, 73–4.
29 Sartre, *Being and Nothingness*, 543.

Coda

1 O'Neill, *Internet Afterlife*.
2 https://www.lifenaut.com, accessed 7 April 2020.
3 https://www.lifenaut.com/mindclone, accessed 7 April 2020.
4 Charlie Brooker, 'San Junipero', *Black Mirror* [TV programme] Dir. Owen Harris (UK: House of Tomorrow, 2016).
5 Leaver, 'Posthumous Performance and Digital Resurrection', 71.
6 The title goes back to David Chalmers, 'Facing Up to the Problem of Consciousness', *Journal of Consciousness Studies* 2, no. 3 (1995): 200–19.
7 Christine Overall, *Aging, Death, and Human Longevity: A Philosophical Inquiry* (Berkeley: University of California Press, 2003), 168–9.
8 Though for some views of consciousness this problem never actually arises: if a computer can carry out the same functions as a normal conscious person, then it *is* conscious. For a discussion of some of the philosophical problems with mind uploading, see David Chalmers 'The Singularity: A Philosophical Analysis', *Journal of Consciousness Studies* 17, nos. 9–10 (2010): 7–65; Massimo Pigliucci, 'Mind Uploading: A Philosophical Counter-Analysis', in *Intelligence Unbound: The Future of Uploaded and Machine Minds*, ed. Russell Blackford and Damien Broderick (Hoboken, NJ: Wiley-Blackwell, 2014), 119–30; Pete Mandik, 'Metaphysical Daring as a Posthuman Survival Strategy' *Midwest Studies in Philosophy* 39, no. 1 (2015): 144–57; Michael Hauskeller, 'My Brain, My Mind, and I: Some Philosophical Problems of Mind-Uploading' *International Journal of Machine Consciousness* 4, no. 1 (2012): 187–200; Patrick D. Hopkins, 'Why Uploading Will Not Work, or, the Ghosts Haunting Transhumanism', *International Journal of Machine Consciousness* 4, no. 1 (2012): 229–43.
9 See e.g. Patrick Stokes, 'Crossing the Bridge: The First-Person and Time', *Phenomenology and the Cognitive Sciences* 13, no. 2 (2014): 295–312; 'Temporal Asymmetry and the Self/Person Split', *Journal of Value Inquiry* 51, no. 2 (2017): 203–19.

Index

abuse 53–4
advertising 44
affordance, 11, 64, 77
afterlife 4, 9, 77, 89
agency 37–9, 133–5, 140
algorithms 74, 151, 153, 157, 158–9
Allen, Woody 84, 87
alterity 100, 150, 154–60
Amazon 158
anchored relationships 44–5, 50, 53
anonymity 43
anticipation 84–5, 87–9, 136, 140, 165
applied ethics 160
Ardern, Jacinda 110
Aristotle 80, 82, 105
Arnold, Michael 78, 139–40
artificial intelligence 2, 46, 137, 139–40, 143, 151, 154, 158–9, 161–2
aspirational identity 49, 71–2
asynchronous communication 64
attention economy 19–20
authenticity 47–50
avatars 2, 34–6, 38–9, 125–8, 130–1, 133, 136–41, 143–4, 151–2, 154, 157, 159, 160–2, 163

Banksy 96
Barthes, Roland 56–7, 64–5, 119, 156–7

Behrendt, Kathy 84
Bell, Alexander Graham 9
Benjamin, Walter 56–7, 64, 82
Beowulf 97, 106–7
Black Mirror, 147–9, 151, 157–60, 164
Blustein, Jeffrey 102, 104–5
bots 43, 124–8, 130, 131–43, 148, 161, 165
boyd, danah 24, 47
Bronzino, Agnolo 56
Brooker, Charlie 147
Brubaker, Jed 115
Buben, Adam 128, 140–3, 157, 161, 181–2 n.42
Buber, Martin 28
Burt, Olivia 23

Calvino, Italo 69–70, 78, 83, 87
Caravaggio, Michelangelo Merisi da 158
Carden, Clarissa 46–7, 79
Carter, Jimmy 38
catfishing 27–8, 172 n.32
Cavell, Stanley 49
Cholbi, Michael 27
Christchurch Massacre 17–18, 110
Chubbuck, Christine 17–18, 19
Clark, Andy 67–8

Clippy (Clippit) 125
closest continuer 136, 148
Cocking, Dean 47
Colvin, Mark 16, 169 n.30
computer-generated imagery (CGI) 129, 159
Confucianism 145
consciousness 15, 28, 72, 82, 88–9, 91, 125, 133–4, 138, 156, 158, 165–6
consignation 118
conspiracy theories 20
continuity 78, 82, 149
corpses, 6, 19, 71, 80, 83, 94, 114
   ambiguity of 56, 82, 156
   care for 79–82, 94
COVID-19 55, 177 n.12
cryonic suspension 90–1
Cushing, Peter 129
cybersex 38
cyberspace 39–41, 45

Daimond, Cora 177 n.8
Davidman, Joy ('H') 100, 144, 149, 156
Davies, Owen 5
dead, the
   ambiguity of 5, 6, 13, 29, 32, 78, 82, 89, 92, 141
   communication with 7–9, 11–12
   commercial value of 73–4, 97–8, 111
   cost to preserve 98–9, 111–12
   interests of 95, 101–4, 112–13, 143
   irreplaceability of 143–4, 157
   at mercy of living 105, 142, 153, 162, 165
   as moral patients 82, 87, 94–5, 101, 105, 112–13
   reality of 31–3, 51
   replacement of 131, 139–45, 154, 157, 160, 164
   as resource 141–3
   speaking for 140, 149–50, 152
Dean, James 129
death
   binary character of 70–1, 89–92
   fear of 84–6, 88–9, 121, 158
   fictional 19–20
   (in)visibility of 17–19, 71, 77–8, 111
   irreversibility of 90–1
   and nonexistence 31–2, 80, 89, 107
   as private 17
   surviving 7, 16, 20, 29, 31, 55, 84, 88–92, 125, 131–2, 163–6
death masks 6, 56, 83
death tech 3, 99
deepfakes 130, 161
deletion 74, 96, 101, 107–9, 113, 120
Derrida, Jacques 118, 140, 142, 149–50, 151, 155–7
digital flesh 6–7, 46–7, 72, 79, 83, 92, 96, 131, 133
digital remains 79, 82–4, 92, 102, 124, 136, 139
   accessibility of 111, 119
   conflicts over 116
   disposal and preservation of 94–5, 102, 106–7, 109–13, 117–20
   legal ownership of 94, 113–17
   vulnerability of 96–101
distance, collapse of 10
Domesday Project 96
doxing 26, 43
Dreyfus, Hubert 15, 59–61
dril. *See* wint
Dwyer, R. Budd 17–18, 19

Index

Ebert, Heidi 99
Edison, Thomas 9
egocentric concern 135–6
Elder, Alexis 141, 145, 161
Electronic Voice Phenomena 10, 168–9 n.21
email 1–3, 41
embodiment 45–7, 53, 61–3, 131
emojis 46
Epicurus 101
Eris (troll) 25–6, 28
ETER9 128
Eterni.Me 127–8, 131, 139, 143, 164
extended cognition 67–8

face (phenomenological concept) 52, 64–5, 72, 88, 92, 155
Facebook 19, 22–3, 44, 49, 50, 72–3, 118
  memorialization 74–6, 77, 78, 87, 94, 97–8, 99, 115, 140
  number of dead users 73, 98
fake deaths 24–9
Feldman, Fred 79
first-person perspective 15, 85–7, 89, 132, 136, 138, 165–6
Fisher, Carrie 129
fission, human 133
fitness trackers 45, 128
Floridi, Luciano 41–2, 61–2, 74, 101, 119
forgetting 14, 98–9, 109–10, 161
Forster, E.M. 58–61, 63, 145
Foucault, Michel 151
four-dimensionalism 178 n.25
Fox Sisters (Margaretta, Catherine, and Leah) 7
Frankenstein 125, 148
Frankfurt, Harry G. 48
Friendster 24

Froese, Jack 1–4, 5, 6, 10, 153
funeral 14–15, 18, 19–20, 22, 59, 71, 83

Gaita, Raimond 81, 109
games 21–22, 25–6, 34–5, 37–8
ghosts 5
Gibson, Belle 25
Gibson, Margaret 33–4, 39, 46–7, 56, 79
Gibson, William 40
GIFs 46
glitches 161–2
God 32
Goethe, Johann Wolfgang von 96
Goffman, Erving 48, 60
Google 13–5, 46, 99
grief 13, 22, 108–9, 144–5, 161
  disenfranchised 22–24
  for nonexistent people 27–9
  parasocial 22–3
  policing of 23
  public 15, 20–24

Hall, Mike 46
Harbinja, Edina 184–5 n.29
Harris, John 112
Harrison, Robert Pogue 80–1, 83, 121
Hartshorne, Charles 31–2
Heersmink, Richard 67–8
Heidegger, Martin 48, 142, 161
Hoff, Carsten 40
Hogan, Bernie 83
Holly, Buddy 129
Houston, Whitney 20, 129
Hughes, Ted 177 n.8

Ibsen, Henrik 82
identity of indiscernibles 132
Ihde, Don 62, 63, 160
immortality 32, 84, 87, 127, 131, 165

impersonation 45, 47. *See also* fake
    deaths, catfishing
Instagram 18, 48, 63
intellectual property 115
Intellitar 127–8, 131
intersubjectivity 51, 87–8, 100

Jang, Ji-sung 130–1
Jang, Nayeon 130–1, 144
Jevin, Gregg (fictional character)
    20–2
Johnston, Mark 84–6
Jürgenson, Friedrich 10, 168–9 n.21

Kant, Immanuel 143
Kasket, Elaine 76–8, 99, 116–17
Keats, John 103–4
Kiel, Paula 99
Kierkegaard, Søren 43, 54, 101,
    104–5, 158
Kim Kierkegaardashian (parody) 43
Kubrick, Stanley 125
Kuyda, Eugenia 123–5, 132

Landsberg, Alison 13
Laurence, Oswald 93
Leaver, Tama 125, 148, 164
Lehner, Nikolaus 19, 158
Leibniz, Gottfried Wilhelm 132
Levinas, Emmanuel, 64, 155
Lewis, C.S. 100, 144, 149–50, 152,
    156
Lewis, David 85
Lifenaut 163–4
Lindemann, Hilde 176 n.52
LinkedIn 50
LiveJournal 24–5
LivesOn 127
livestreaming 17–18
Locke, John 133
Lucretius 31

machine learning 137–39
MacIntyre, Alasdair 35, 51
make-believe 12
Marjorie Prime 139
Marx, Karl 74
Matrix, The 40
Mayer-Schönberger, Viktor 98
Mazurenko, Roman 123–5, 128, 144,
    148, 153
McCollum, Margaret 93
McCulloch, Gretchen 46
McManus, Ruth 68
media richness theory 63–4
mediation 19–20, 53–5, 56, 60
memorialisation, public 110–11
memory, organic 101, 106, 150
mental imagery 152
Merleau-Ponty, Maurice 62
mesmerism 8
Microsoft 99
Mike (chicken) 91
mind uploading 163–6
Minecraft 21
Minsky, Marvin 177 n.15
Morse, Samuel 7–8, 9, 154
mourning practices 14–15, 145
    online 20–4, 25, 75–7, 94, 99
Mumler, William 9
Munch, Edvard 152
Munchausen syndrome 26–7
MySpace 31, 45, 73, 76

Nagel, Thomas 81, 132
narrative identity 35, 37, 38–9, 48–9,
    51, 90
Nipper (*His Master's Voice* dog) 10,
    176 n.10
nonymity 44
Norlock, Karthyn 176 n.52
Nozick, Robert 136, 148
Nussbaum, Martha 188 n.39

O'Neill, Kevin 88, 163
Oderberg, David 1–3, 4
offline social reasoning 77
Öhman, Carl 73, 74, 101
onlife 41–2
Onlife Manifesto, The 41–2
online
    as communicative status 41–2
    as unreal 20, 24, 29, 33–4, 38, 43, 45, 47–51, 53
    as unserious 18, 20
Ostritsch, Sebastian 38
Otsuchi 10–12
Overall, Christine 165
overwriting 6, 19, 99–101, 119–20, 150–1

Palladino, Eusapia 69
Parfit, Derek 135
Parker, Alison and Adam Ward, murder of 20
Patterson, Chastity 76–7
Pearson, Erika 45
Pepper's Ghost illusion 129
person/self distinction 15, 66, 86–7, 136
personal identity 16, 27, 34–5, 66–8, 82, 133–6, 137
personhood 34, 66–7, 133–4
    distributed 65–8, 87, 105
phenomenality 6, 13, 55, 119
phenomenology 53, 62, 82
Phillips, Whitney 24, 45
Philosophy 15, 160
    of death, 16, 32, 81–2, 101–2
photography
    portrait 6, 56–7, 64, 139, 188 n.30
    spirit 9
pile-ons 54
portraiture 13, 56

Powell, Lewis (aka Lewis Paine) 56–7, 139
Pristas, Randy 46
privacy 114–15, 116–17
prop 12
prosthetic memory 13, 67
Purmont, Aaron 12–13
Purmont, Nora McInerney 12–13

Quan-Haase, Anabel 83
Queen Victoria Market 95

reanimation 7, 132, 136, 139, 140, 143, 147, 152, 158
recollection, 141–2, as duty 104–6, 108–9, 140, 154
Reddit 17
Renaudo, Ben 78
Replika 124, 132
Ricoeur, Paul 35, 89–90
Right to be forgotten (*Costeja* case), 13–14
Rogue One 129
Roland, Francis 7
Rothblatt, Martine 163–4

Samoa, attitudes to death 19
Sartre, Jean-Paul 152, 155, 162
Sasaki, Itaru 10–11
Savile, Jimmy 109–11
Schechtman, Marya 34–7, 38, 86
Schopenhauer, Arthur 158
Schreiber, Benjamin 91
Sconce, Jeffrey 7, 9
Second Life 33–6, 38–9, 42, 46
selfies 18
server failure 97
Short Message Service (SMS) 64, 76–7, 128
Skype. *See* video calling
Sparrow, Jeff 170 n.2

Spiritualism 7–9, 78, 168n13
spontaneity 62, 134, 153, 157–60, 189 n.21
standing reserve 142
Star Trek 137
Steiner, Peter 43
Stoppard, Tom 85, 87
suicide 17, 26

Taylor, James Stacey 105
Te'o, Manti 28–9
technology,
    novelty, 7, 41
    obsolescence 96–7
    transparency of 6, 58, 62–3, 161–2
telegraph 7, 64
telephone 9, 11, 63, 64
telepresence 55, 58, 59–63, 154, 177 n.15
telic possibility 2–4, 6, 43, 131, 153, 167n.2
Terasem Foundation 163–4
termination thesis 79
Thompson, Janna 103
TikTok 19
time, effect of internet on 13–14
Torajan death practices 71–2, 83
transhumanism 125, 163–4
trolling 23–4, 45
Tupac Shakur 129

Turing Test 159, 161
Twitter 16, 20–1, 40, 42, 43, 94, 97, 126, 127

uncanny valley 127
Unidentified Flying Objects 5
Ursache, Marius 128
Ussing, Susanne 40
utilitarianism 112

van den Hoven, Jeroen 47
van Dijck José 44, 49
Velleman, J. David 19, 38
video calling 55, 59, 64
Virtual Eternity. *See* Intellitar

Walton, Kendall 12
Watson, David 73, 101
West, Kanye 133
Whitman, Walt 8–9, 176 n.15
will, 85–6, 94, 140
Wind Phone 10–12, 77
wint (Twitter personality) 43

Yourgrau, Palle 31–2, 81
YouTube 18, 22

Zhao, Shenyang 48
Zoom. *See* video calling
Zuckerberg, Mark 44

www.ingramcontent.com/pod-product-compliance
Lightning Source LLC
Chambersburg PA
CBHW051811230426
43672CB00012B/2694